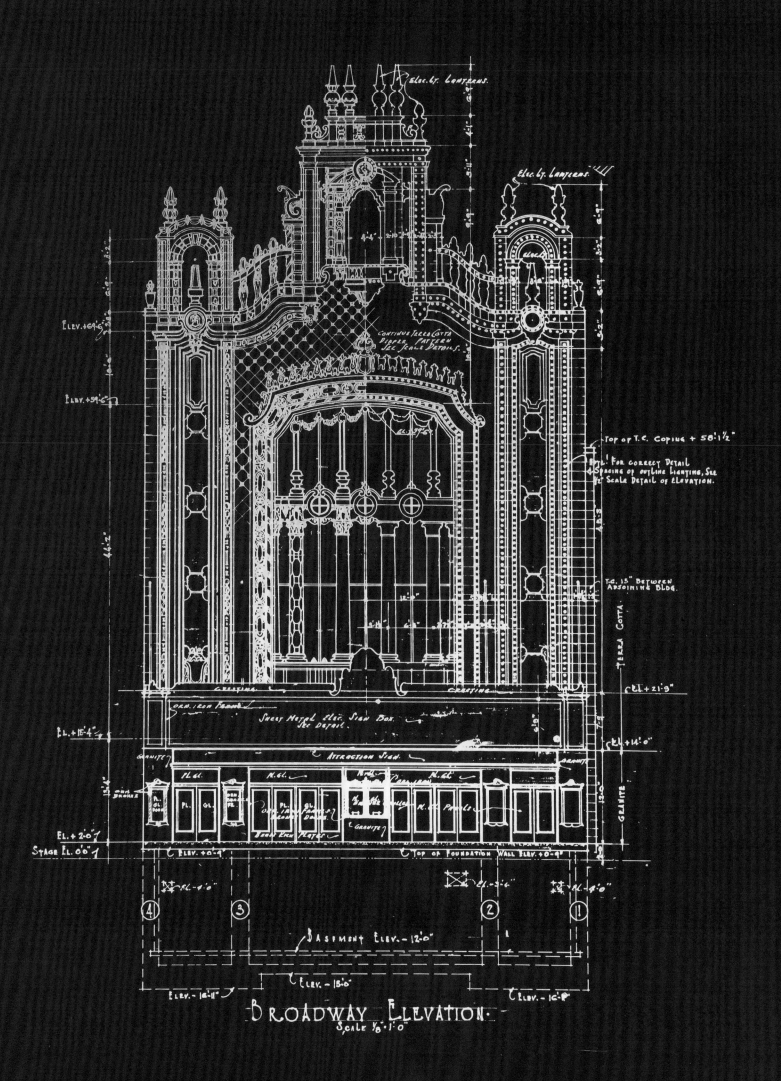

THE UPTOWN
CHICAGO'S ENDANGERED MOVIE PALACE

ROBERT LOERZEL   JAMES A. PIERCE

FEATURING PHOTOGRAPHS BY

RICHARD CAHAN
CHRISTOPHER JACKSON
BARBARA KARANT
PAUL MERIDETH
JACK MILLER
MARK MONTGOMERY

PAUL NATKIN
ERIC J. NORDSTROM
SUZY POLING
CAREY PRIMEAU
LOREN ROBARE
LESLIE SCHWARTZ

CITYFILES PRESS

Copyright © 2025 CityFiles Press
All rights reserved. No part
of this book may be reproduced
in any form without permission
in writing from the publisher.

FIRST EDITION

ISBN-13: 978-1-7338690-7-2

Printed in China

Produced and designed by Michael Williams
Edited by Richard Cahan
Introduction © James A. Pierce
Text © Robert Loerzel
Images © Individual photographers

Endsheets: : C.W. & Geo. L. Rapp rendering
Page 1: Facade blueprint
Pages 2-3: Chicago Architectural Photographing Company
Pages 4-5: Paul Merideth photos
Pages 6-7: Barbara Karant photos
Pages 8-9: Suzy Poling photos
Page 10: Barbara Karant photo
Pages 12-13: Richard Cahan photo

This publication is made possible through support from the Richard H. Driehaus Foundation.

CONTENTS

INTRODUCTION 14
James A. Pierce

THE UPTOWN
Robert Loerzel

GRAND OPENING 18
BACKSTORY 60
CONSTRUCTION 76
A TEMPLE OF ENTERTAINMENT 94
CHANGING TIMES 110
THE ROCK ERA 124
IN LIMBO 138

NOTES ON SOURCES 166

ACKNOWLEDGMENTS 168

Introduction

JAMES A. PIERCE

The Uptown Theatre—a movie palace built "for all time"—must be saved.

Opened exactly one hundred years ago, and shuttered in 1981, the Uptown is the largest, most elaborate movie theater of its era still standing. With grand lobbies, sweeping stairways and more than 4,300 seats, the Uptown was advertised as "another world" when it opened in 1925. A century later, it still is. For many, the Uptown is a sacred space.

In 1960, preservationist Richard Nickel took to the streets of downtown Chicago to protest the demolition of a similarly vaunted theater, the Garrick. He carried a sign that asked: "Do We Dare Squander Chicago's Great Architectural Heritage?"

Nickel's question remains.

The Uptown, at 4816 North Broadway in Chicago's North Side neighborhood of the same name, would be too costly to tear down and very expensive to restore. And there are too many challenges now for it to be open to the public. That's why we created this book. We want people to see it and learn its stories. We want people to figure out how Chicago and the nation can save this massive architectural jewel. We believe these photos and this history will rekindle the will to save the Uptown.

We hope it's not a last look.

This is more than a history. It's a document that puts on record the story of a cultural icon that survived to serve a succession of popular, large-scale amusements (silent movies, stage shows, talkies, and concerts) and persevered. It's an account of the Uptown neighborhood that will rise or level off depending on the theater's fate. And it's a detailed description of the theater's construction, opening days, glory years, and decades of challenges.

It's also a plea. To glean from the past and imagine the future. We hope readers will rediscover the Uptown and agree it can once again be a cultural magnet to better the Uptown neighborhood and Chicago.

Can the Uptown be saved? There *is* precedent. The more-than-5,000-seat Fox Theatre in Detroit was restored and given a new life in 1988. Chicago's Oriental Theatre (now the Nederlander) was dark for seventeen years before being restored for $35 million and reopened. And the Kings Theatre in Brooklyn, abandoned in 1977, reopened in 2015 after a $95 million campaign. Each of these theaters plays host to live performances almost every night.

Our beloved theater awaits its next act.

The Uptown Theatre is shrouded in myth that outsizes its colossus.

Unscalable in size, impenetrable in darkness, and guarded securely, it remains what *Newcity* magazine calls "the best theater in Chicago you can't see," as it has been for more than forty years. Even though it fills most of a city block and towers over neighboring buildings, the Uptown has been closed for so long it's almost invisible.

It is a top-tier Chicago landmark hiding in plain sight.

Since it's open only occasionally—for tours, special events, or as a TV and movie location—being inside the Uptown is on the bucket list for many Chicagoans.

When I began giving Saturday tours of the

Left: The "Uptown Community Portrait 2000" event celebrated the theater's 75th anniversary.
MARK MONTGOMERY PHOTO

Uptown as a 26-year-old in 1998, it was not uncommon to meet people with vivid memories of going to "the show" for movies and concerts. During tours, many wistfully said, "I hope to see it restored before I die."

That hope remains.

The Uptown occupies a unique place. It was busy and profitable from its heyday of three shows a day until the theater, worn but still glamorous, played host to legendary rock concerts. Tens of millions of people enjoyed the Uptown. No other venue of this vintage, size, and quality has remained shuttered for so long without being restored, demolished, radically altered, or reconfigured. The Uptown is on the brink. It's one of the most enigmatic historic preservation challenges of our lifetime.

How perverse it is that the Uptown now hosts only a few volunteers and tradespeople who walk across its quiet marble floors to do subsistence maintenance. So much so that the "phantom" caretakers of the Uptown are people of local lore.

Like other keepers of the theater, I learned to appreciate the Uptown through Theatre Historical Society of America, a group founded in the late 1960s which created a network of fans who document and celebrate great, old theaters across America. It opened my eyes.

Joe DuciBella, a founding member of the organization, was a key mentor. He grew up on Chicago's West Side, frequented the Paradise (torn down in the 1950s) and the Marbro (demolished in the 1960s), and worked as an usher at the Uptown. He became the theater's leading authority.

DuciBella deplored the destruction of movie palaces. "The problem is really that the best are gone," he wrote in 1987. "Perhaps one could debate which movie theatres were the 'best.' But what the public—the real judge, in the end—liked best and tried to save were, in most instances, a select few of the thousands of theatres built primarily to show movies."

That's why the Uptown is so valuable.

I began to feel a dramatic contradiction between downtown and Uptown in the 1990s as I would go from ushering at the plush and popular Oriental, Chicago, and Auditorium theaters to checking on and doing small chores at the eerily quiet, dark and uncarpeted Uptown. Only the distant sound of planes headed to O'Hare, or the nearby "L" and buses interrupted the continuous performance of silence.

It was never truly abandoned, but only a few owners since its doors closed have advanced serious plans for its future use or worked to assemble financing for its restoration. A succession of long-serving volunteers has worked with each owner or receiver to safeguard and stabilize the building. Alongside having their own careers, the volunteers have invested much of their free time keeping the building viable. The work, often at night and on weekends, is dirty, cold and wet. The hours were long.

These "Friends of the Uptown" often paid for parts and supplies from their own pockets. They bartered their labor so that the nonprofit organization they created—the Landmark Uptown Theatre Corporation—could acquire and safeguard the Uptown's original bronze and crystal Victor S. Pearlman & Company chandeliers for eventual restoration and re-installation in the theater.

This long history of volunteer work began at the theater in secret in 1975, when the Uptown was closed briefly for some TLC. The last man standing after it closed in 1981 was retired Plitt Theatres projectionist Phil Bohmann, who refused to walk away and let the Uptown fall to ruin without appealing for help. Lacking heat and maintenance, the Uptown suffered monumental damage during bitter cold 1980s winters, making it impossible to open again without extensive restoration.

Through the following decades, the Uptown has had just a few guardians, including Bob Boin, Curt Mangel, Dan Sanders, Dave Syfczak, Jimmy Wiggins, myself, and others. We've responded to emergencies and helped keep the building viable for tours and inspections. Check-ins on the theater could be shocking. Sometimes we found the Uptown standing in water. At other times frozen in ice.

Its darkest day perhaps came during a winter

blast in early 2005. Syfczak couldn't heat the Uptown because the supply of No. 5 oil needed to fuel the boiler had run out—and no owner or partner would return his calls. The building was ice-cold, the water standing in the sump pump was frozen, and the risk was growing that the main freshwater supply pipe would freeze, explode, and flood the basement's mechanical rooms.

Syfczak sat alone on the tiled curving stair beneath the Grand Lobby. He felt hopeless, but resolved to keep vigil, using a torpedo kerosene space heater and a small torch to warm the city water main little by little overnight and through the next frigid week. It was long enough to avert catastrophe. When an owner eventually responded, Syfczak ordered the oil and started the 29-step process of priming, warming, and firing up the boiler. The loud water hammer sound began as steam reached the far perimeter radiators along the theater's exterior walls and above the auditorium. Disaster was averted for another day.

Working as a "Friend of the Uptown" was not always fraught with trouble. We helped give tours, hosted special events and weddings, prepared for TV and film shoots, and assisted crews that built high-quality light and sound shows for the annual gay men's "Hearts Parties," also known as circuit parties. These Valentine's Day events attracted 2,000 dancers and many top-name performers.

Looking back, it's funny how little time we spent in the biggest room in the building; most things that needed attention were on the perimeter or in the mechanical rooms. We scrubbed and painted over graffiti, checked that all 110 doors were locked, cleared debris from the roof drains, replaced lightbulbs from atop a 26-foot ladder, kept the one shopworn boiler blasting, and made sure all the floors were as clean and dry as possible. At times, we realized we were patching our own patches, using hydraulic cement to seal large cracks and holes in steel roof drains that had been cracked open by ice. The Uptown's twelve roof surfaces drain to the basement through a system of pipes connecting with the city sewer. The failure of this system in winter funneled rain and snowmelt into the interior, ruining large sections of ornate plaster ceilings and walls.

Volunteers have played a major role in what is the building's last, best chance. We've always worked with the expectation that the Uptown will be saved. After pulling down a ragged curtain from the Grand Lobby window on a frigid February afternoon, I asked founding volunteer Curt Mangel, called the original Phantom of the Uptown, if we should save the fabric. "No," he replied. "It will be replaced when the restoration happens." His word "when" was the key. No emphasis. No sarcasm. We made it clear: "If" would never be spoken.

Every once in a while, we were asked to give tours to promote the Uptown. A little paint here, some new plaster there, mopping and buffing the floor, and getting rid of junk made the theater look like a million bucks. Each time Bob Boin or Dave Syfczak opened the barricade door to a different investor, architect, promoter, banker, or hanger-on, guests were given an enthusiastic and colorful excursion through the building in the hope that it would make a difference. We held demolition by neglect at bay. Without our dedication and work, the Uptown would already be gone. And people would be asking, "How did we let that happen?"

But without restoration and use, the Uptown remains at risk. My generation saw what happened in 1989 when Chicago signed off on the demolition of the historic Granada Theatre movie palace about two miles north.

The small but mighty Friends of the Uptown continues to work to keep the idea of restoring the Uptown alive by preserving the best of what makes the theater so rare. This book is part of that effort. Restoring the Uptown must be an act of altruism. It will never pencil out. The project requires significant private and public funding. Its plight is increasingly urgent because restoration costs continue to climb.

The Uptown's myth—like the steel, concrete, brick, terra cotta, and marble forming its physical structure—carries immense substance and weight. Hard work has delivered the building to today and kept it ready for revival.

But as this book reveals, the time to save the Uptown is now.

CHAPTER ONE

GRAND OPENING

'We are in wonderland.'

An original drawing of the Uptown Theatre auditorium by C.W. & Geo. L. Rapp, Architects.

"It outdoes your dreams," the advertisements declared. "IT WILL HUSH AND THRILL YOU. It throbs with beauty—lovely enough to hold the heart of a woman all her life. You will love it. ... An enchanted palace—a house of magic beauty. ... Great and beautiful as a magic city— AN ACRE OF SEATS under a romantic and color-lit twilight from myriads of unseen lamps. ... One of the great art-buildings of the world—and in it, room for everybody! ... It opens Tuesday! ... an event you will remember all your life."

It may have sounded like a lot of hyperbole, but nearly everyone who stepped inside Balaban & Katz's Uptown Theatre for its grand opening events on August 17 and 18, 1925, agreed: It truly was an astounding work of architecture and art, rendered on an immense scale. One of the largest cinemas ever constructed, the Uptown was a shining pinnacle of a golden age for movies as well as movie theaters—an era when the city of Chicago led the world in a building boom of the astonishingly large and excessively lavish structures that came to be known as movie palaces. And more than anyone else, the men of Balaban & Katz were the kings of these castles. These ambitious masters of showmanship and construction had already opened four magnificent theaters across the city over the previous eight years, all designed by Chicago architects Rapp & Rapp: the Central Park Theatre on the West Side, the Riviera on the North Side, the Tivoli on the South Side, and the Chicago Theatre in the heart of the Loop. And now they'd turned their attention back to the North Side's Uptown neighborhood and constructed their biggest theater of all, just northwest of Lawrence Avenue and Broadway— right across the street from the Riviera.

On the night of Saturday, August 15, the building's signs were switched on, including the 12-foot-high letters with 925 light bulbs on the roof announcing "UPTOWN THEATRE," as well as the word "UPTOWN" spelled vertically on the front of the building. With its buff, or light-yellow, brick walls, the massive L-shaped structure nestled around the two-story Green Mill Gardens building at the corner. Light bulbs traced the contours of the Uptown's 104-foot-high terra cotta façade facing Broadway, where steel-and-glass lanterns crowned the spires. Above the theater's marquee, four columns stood in front of a grand window. Higher up, a Spanish-style arch was topped by a gentle curve, with concave indents on its corners. "Hundreds of thousands of incandescent lamps ... were switched on simultaneously for the first time last night," the *Chicago Daily Tribune* announced. "The radiance of the huge electric signs on the theater ... was reported to be visible over most of the North Side."

The *Chicago Daily News* reported interior decorators put their final touches on the theater at midnight as Sunday came to an end, but other reports indicated their work was far from complete. "The great lobby was cluttered with debris," wrote Harold H. Green, who stopped inside at 10 a.m. on Monday, August 17, when the Uptown was being readied to host a "dress rehearsal" preview show for invited guests, the night before it would open to the public. "Many of the seats were still missing, lamp sockets were empty, many of the stage settings were in the orchestra circle, and hundreds of men were running wildly about, apparently seeing how much dust they could kick up," Green wrote.

He was visiting from Cleveland, where he worked as the advertising manager of the General Electric Company's National Lamp Works. Reporting on the Uptown's opening for his company's magazine *Light*, Green couldn't believe it would be ready in time. But he saw Barney Balaban, one of the top executives at Balaban & Katz, "chatting and smiling and looking as fresh and pink as though he had risen from a long night's sleep to enjoy a peaceful holiday." Balaban assured him that everything would be set. As the reporter surveyed the building, he found an electrician who had been knocked out by a falling bolt. And before going to lunch, Green observed: "In the balcony a squad of young men in shirt sleeves were lined up like West Point cadets on parade. They were ushers, getting their instructions."

Rapp & Rapp's drawing of the Grand Lobby depicts what a Chicago newspaper called a "Palace of Dreams."

A 1925 ad promotes the beauty of the theater.

This was a marvelous place.

As a week of celebratory festivities began in the Uptown neighborhood, Balaban & Katz invited city officials, VIPs, and journalists to Monday night's preview, as well as the workers who had labored on the building. They were encouraged to bring along their wives and families. Five thousand guests reportedly attended—hundreds more than the number of available seats—while throngs of people without invitations gathered outside, hoping they might get an early peek.

A *Variety* reporter wrote that the theater was far from finished: "Many of the staircases were uncarpeted and without banisters. The box office had no windows or other equipment installed … and there were ladders and tools scattered about in all sorts of corners. Workmen in overalls were numerously present." But Green, who had witnessed disarray that morning, was amazed by how much the Uptown had been transformed in a half day. At 7:30 that night, he walked up Broadway with his family. "As we approached Lawrence, things took on a festive air," he wrote.

"Strings of colored lights stretched across the streets, lamp posts were gaily trimmed and flags waved everywhere. The number of people on the streets reminded one of an election night before prohibition."

Uptown has probably never been as crowded as it was during that week in August 1925, when three-quarters of a million people reportedly turned out for six days of festivities. Six miles north of downtown Chicago, the neighborhood had sprouted from a rural countryside over the previous three decades. It was a city within the city, complete with bustling shops, hotels, nightclubs, and theaters. And now, as Uptown welcomed the opening of a gigantic movie theater, people danced in the streets and bands played on the corners, while daredevil Joseph O. Flory repeatedly set himself on fire atop a nearby building, performing "The Dive of Death" into a small tank of water.

Green was stunned by the sight of the Uptown Theatre's massive white letters illuminated against the dark sky. "The beautiful white front of the building was outlined in light, and under the marquee the brightness would have shamed the sun," he wrote. "The impossible had happened: the Uptown was opening on schedule." Across the marquee, milk glass letters spelled out messages in white words against a dark surface: "AN ACRE OF SEATS IN A MAGIC CITY … ONE OF THE GREAT ART BUILDINGS OF THE WORLD."

Green was even more astounded by what he saw as he walked through the theater's bronze doors on Broadway, stepping into a series of lobbies that stretched westward for an entire city block. The first of these rooms was the Grand Lobby, 100 feet long and 60 feet wide topped by a coffered and frescoed ceiling 64 feet above the marble floor. "Do you think you could describe the beauty of a rose to one who had never seen a rose?" Green wrote. "I feel as lost now in attempting to describe this vision from old Spain."

In the years ahead, countless people would experience the same sensation of breathtaking wonder when they went through those doors.

"Entering it you pass into another world," wrote the *Balaban & Katz Magazine,* a promotional publication that put out a special issue dedicated to the Uptown. "The streets, the clangor of iron on cement, the harsh outlines of the steel thickets we call the city, all disappear. Your spirit rises and soars along the climbing pillars that ascend six stories to the dome ceiling of the colossal lobby." Travertine marble, imported from Italy specially for the Uptown, covered many of the Grand Lobby's surfaces. Rapp & Rapp's chief designer, Arthur Frederick Adams, said this material, with its beautiful irregularities, helped to create the illusion that the Uptown was a palace in Seville, Barcelona, or Madrid.

When *Chicago Evening Post* writer H. Campbell-Duncan walked in, he was "thrilled by the orgy of expenditure displayed on every side," remarking: "Money seems to have been poured out like water to make the Uptown Theatre the last word in cinema palace gorgeousness." The *Chicago Evening American's* Rob Reel thought it looked like a "larger, grander and more golden" version of the Chicago Theatre's lobby. The room was banked with floral arrangements—tributes from the hundreds of companies that had constructed and outfitted the Uptown, as well as hundreds of other well-wishers.

Anyone entering this space would have noticed the air inside the Uptown Theatre was cooler than the air out on Broadway. The weather was warmer than usual for mid-August. Chicagoans had come to expect the refreshing coolness of air conditioning when they came to see movies during the summer at Balaban & Katz theaters. Over the previous several years, the company had opened some of the world's first theaters with air conditioning, including the Central Park, the Riviera, the Tivoli, and the Chicago. During hot weather, advertisements showed the names of these theaters capped by snow and dripping with icicles. "Balaban & Katz Theatres keep you utterly comfortable with their giant freezing plants," said one ad. Another simply stated: "It's cool here." This was a major lure in an

The Uptown's opening week program in 1925.

era when no homes had air conditioning. Balaban & Katz touted the Chicago health commissioner's advice that people should go to the movies so they could breathe fresh air. As the Uptown opened, B&K's magazine said the building contained "complex yet never-failing machinery that you never see, shining engines that change the air in the theater every two minutes, wash the air, cool the air, rewash the air, temper it exactly to your comfort."

At the Grand Lobby's far end, two sets of stairs curved up to a promenade—a mezzanine-level walkway with bronze railings along the sides of the space, where paintings hung on the silk damask panel walls. Patrons were free to stroll the promenade, looking at the art. The promenade's eastern side—above the Broadway entrance doors—was a Musicians' Gallery alongside the façade's 30-foot-high grand window, where string quartets and other small ensembles would perform.

In spite of the lobby's marble and plaster surfaces, the room did not fill with echoes. Sound was absorbed by padding on the promenade walls, hidden behind the damask.

The grandest things about the Grand Lobby may have been the piers holding up the promenade and the columns that ascended to the ceiling. Six of these ornate vertical structures were arrayed on either side of the room, giving the space a sense of extreme importance. Each pier featured gilt-clad plaster castings of women. Higher up, other intriguing details caught the eye, as the *Balaban & Katz Magazine* described: "the fanciful heads of Renaissance cupids, fantastic gargoyles, griffins, the laughing heads of mythological gods and jolly demons grimace in friendly humor from the entablatures about the tops of the pillars."

Looking up, patrons saw three giant chandeliers, each containing more than 200 light bulbs. Custom-designed by the Chicago firm Victor S. Pearlman & Company, with crystal baskets and a motif of dripping icicles, the fixtures cost $10,000 each in 1925. (To adjust for inflation, multiply all 1925 dollar figures by eighteen to get the 2025 equivalent.) At nighttime, when the drapes on the Broadway façade's window opened, people could see the glitter of those chandeliers from out on the street. Gold, red, and blue colors were applied to the ceiling's aluminum leaf surface. "The aluminum leaf surface is used to intensify the light rays which will be projected from concealed lights behind the crested cornice," wrote Adams, the chief of design.

Some moviegoers enjoyed lingering in the Grand Lobby or other foyers—and they were allowed to do so. "Do not disturb patrons who are obviously roaming about the foyer or lobby promenades for the purpose of inspecting the decorations, or enjoying the spaciousness and comfort of our theatres," Balaban & Katz told its ushers. "We have purposely provided many attractions there for their entertainment and have invited and encouraged them to make these inspections." Except, of course, during busy times.

As the *Evening Post's* H. Campbell-Duncan wandered through the Uptown, ushers seemed to be everywhere. That wasn't surprising, considering how large the theater's staff was—131 employees in all, including twenty-three ushers and fourteen other service staff members. "At each corner and turn I encountered crimson-uniformed ushers and attendants ready to give me courteous directions and information," Campbell-Duncan wrote. "They were everywhere and at a distance appeared like flaming hibiscus blossoms splashed against the deeper tones of rich hangings and mural decorations."

Balaban & Katz provided plenty of objects for people to gaze upon. Every nook and cranny—even the bathrooms—had decorative elements: hand-carved marble, colored glass windows, mural paintings, spires and minarets, bronze French clocks, Spanish oil jars, as well as tapestries and jeweled ornaments from France and Italy. The *Balaban & Katz Magazine* promised: "In all the house, stand where you will, your eye can rest on nothing but beauty."

Beyond providing space to display all of this decor and art, the Uptown's vast lobbies also served a practical purpose: As thousands sat in the auditorium watching a show, thousands of others could wait comfortably until it was their turn. Covering 46,000 square feet, the Uptown was said to contain twice as much "holdout space" as the Chicago Theatre. And the building's L shape provided an efficient system for getting people out of the theater quickly. People entered from Broadway, moving west and then heading south into the auditorium, the bulk of the building that extended to Lawrence Avenue. When a show was over, they went either south (exiting onto Lawrence) or west (exiting onto Magnolia Avenue). This creative layout allowed for the movement of nearly 9,000 people in and out of the Uptown within just fifteen minutes.

Standing in the Grand Lobby and looking

Right: Patrons line up for opening day on August 18, 1925. This photo and the following photos in this chapter were all taken by the Chicago Architectural Photographing Company.

First view of the Uptown Theatre's Grand Lobby. Left: Looking east back toward the entrance.

toward the stairs, one could glimpse the theater's depths. "The effect of vista … is one of terraced grandeur, with elliptical stairways on each side receding into the distant mezzanine and balcony floors," wrote designer Adams.

Men waiting near the Grand Lobby's staircase might take another set of stairs down to the basement's lounge, also known as the "smoking room," a Gothic-style chamber with backlit stained-glass windows, a faux fireplace, heavy oak furniture, and two suits of standing armor. The rest of the basement was off-limits to the public, but an ad offered an enticing description of what lay hidden there: "Behind this grandeur, in the tremendous cellars, sub-cellars and concealed recesses as well as backstage, are innumerable ingenious and intricate devices of modern invention working silently and mysteriously to provide bewitching theatrical effects, as well as to give you every comfort of your own home." There were workspaces for electricians, carpenters, janitors, and "scrub women," along with a locker room and club room for the ushers, a storage room for entertainers' trunks, and a library for the orchestra's sheet music. And a maze of basement chambers was filled with ducts, pipes, fans, and other machinery that kept the building cool in the summer and warm in the winter, including two high-pressure carbon dioxide air cooling units, each weighing 200 tons, and three cylindrical boilers the size of locomotives.

At the base of the Grand Lobby's staircase, the captain of the ushers kept an eye on a device called the seating indicator, an ornate metal box with vertical rows of circular lights that received signals from ushers around the theater. Whenever a section of seats filled up, the corresponding light on the box went dark, helping the captain decide where the ushers should escort the next set of patrons to the best remaining seats. Another indicator sat near the cashier, so that she knew when to stop selling tickets.

Ushers took some guests up the stairs into the Great Hall, a carpeted 60-by-29-foot space that served as a sort of crossroads. From here, people could walk through an arch into the auditorium's mezzanine level, also known as the loge, and sit for the show. Or they could continue up another grand staircase to the balcony. Here, another arch led to a corridor running south toward Lawrence Avenue.

But the Great Hall was not just a functional junction for pedestrian traffic. Like so many rooms in the Uptown, it offered beauty to behold. The walls were covered with walnut veneer paneling, stretching up 30 feet. Above that, frescoed panels of cherubs and griffins were topped by a heavy cornice. Two chandeliers hung from the plaster ceiling. And paintings of Spanish noblemen and knights were set in arched niches above the staircase's first rise. "Richly colored beams as from old Spanish inns stretch across the inner lobbies, gigantic mural paintings fill arches and coves," the *Balaban & Katz Magazine* noted.

Back in the Grand Lobby, some guests took another route into the auditorium—staying on the ground floor and walking straight west beneath

Colonnades gleam on both sides of the theater lobby. Left: A sweeping staircase rises to the mezzanine.

the staircase. This way led into the Fountain Lobby, a low-ceilinged 60-by-60-foot area where a fountain—made of black marble and scagliola, an imitation marble made from plaster—stood flanked by gilt thrones. Overhead lights cast colors onto fish and lilies in the mosaic-tile-lined basin. Florists would compete to display their arrangements under these shifting color spotlights.

Like the Great Hall space above it, the Fountain Lobby was a crossroads. One could turn south, where a corridor sloped down toward Lawrence Avenue, or head west into the Grand Foyer.

The tall Grand Foyer, also known as the Magnolia Lobby, extends 84 feet along the auditorium's rear wall. It reaches 40 feet high to a timbered, stenciled ceiling, which had three bronze

Looking across the Grand Lobby from the Musicians' Gallery on the mezzanine level.

The mezzanine promenade above the Grand Lobby is a gallery of paintings and sculpture.

cage-like chandeliers. From this foyer, ushers would turn left, guiding moviegoers toward their seats, passing through four sets of wide, bronze French doors. One floor above, people on the mezzanine level could walk on a promenade, where arches gave them views overlooking the lobby.

The Grand Foyer's plaster castings include seashells above the promenade arches. Each of those half-shells is topped by a grotesque face—a man with an intense expression, his mouth wide open revealing his teeth. A nearly naked boy sits on top of that head, with his legs casually draped to one side. The boy holds a festoon of flowers. The shape of the arches here echoes the building's

One last look at the Grand Lobby. Left: A stair landing in the Great Hall leads to the upper levels.

façade on Broadway: a gently curving line at the top, with concave indents on both corners. It's a motif that repeats throughout the building.

In contrast with the marble floors near the building's entrance, the Grand Foyer and other areas near the auditorium had carpeting, which muffled sound. It's believed that Rapp & Rapp designed the carpet—a bay leaf torus molding crosshatch over a William Morris pattern with two shades of burgundy. As H. Campbell-Duncan strolled around the building in 1925, he walked over "an acre or so of Oriental Rugs with a depth of pile that gave the effect of walking upon moss."

Alongside the Grand Foyer, the ladies' lounge

The lounge area of the Grand Foyer.

was a small oval French Rococo–inspired space where four corner glass niches held Dresden china figurines. That led into the powder room, with its makeup tables, mirrors, and toilets. A nursery was nearby, where children could amuse themselves on a carousel and a rocking horse. The walls were painted with pictures of clowns, tin soldiers, a monkey, Jack climbing his magic beanstalk, and a Roman soldier riding a chariot.

Most guests headed south from the Grand Foyer into the auditorium, where they found themselves under a low ceiling at the back of the 2,282-seat main floor. The mezzanine or loge level was over their heads. Rows of lights on the side of aisle seats beckoned them down these walkways. The soft diffused glow from the lights were both pleasing and practical. Wrote Harold Green, in *Light* magazine: "There is no groping blindly down the aisle to end up in the lap of an indignant stranger."

As guests continued walking forward, the mezzanine's overhang ended and they entered a

The Grand Foyer provides entrances to the auditorium. Ushers opened curtained doors into the theater.

space where the balcony's soffit was 18 feet above their heads, angled slightly upward to offer a fuller view of the stage. And if they kept moving forward, they passed into an area where the balcony no longer blocked their view of the domed ceiling. Here, they would finally get a sense of just how vast the auditorium is.

As Green looked around, he noted how the Uptown's complex lighting system cast various colors. "The walls are painted with a rosy pink light that is new and different," he observed. "The kind of light that gives real pleasure with its translucent glow, a light that penetrates but does not dazzle. Nowhere in the illuminating of the interior of this theater is white light used. The hanging ceiling of the auditorium is a thing that artists will enthuse over. By suspending a portion of the ceiling, lights from unseen coves are thrown

The doors at left lead to the mezzanine seats of the immense auditorium.

on the rest, giving it the appearance of a pearl-coated shell, and the design at the border of the suspended portion is thus thrown into relief."

The auditorium's dome has three levels. The lowest looks like it's floating on a bed of light, guarded by seated griffins holding shields. The griffins, mythical creatures used by architects as a sign of protection, seem tiny from the main floor. But from the back of the balcony, patrons could see they were 7 feet tall. Sweeping around three sides of the auditorium, an ornate wall-like structure rises behind the griffins, with beam-like ribs and backlit Spanish windows. Difficult to discern from a distance, the crowned heads of kings jut from this structure's mass of ornamental shapes. Seen up close from the balcony, the monarchs appear to be laughing, but dramatic shadows cover their sharply angled eyes and mouths.

This men's lounge was also known as the "smoking room." Left: The mezzanine level of the Grand Foyer.

Above, the dome's next level has a simpler surface of heavy stucco. And in the middle, an opening reveals the dome's top level, a rounded rectangle of stucco. Depending on the lighting, this central piece of the dome appears to be a window open to the night sky. When the *Evening Post's* H. Campbell-Duncan gazed up, he saw softly modulated lights playing across the dome like the aurora borealis. At its high point, the dome was 95 feet above street level, while the auditorium's main floor sloped down to 6 feet below the street.

Anyone who happened to wander up to the auditorium's top level, where the projectionist's "kinobooth" was located, would have gotten a stunning view of the auditorium, looking down on the sprawling 1,638-seat balcony. Someone looking from this vantage might think they were near the top of the building, but they were actually still about 45 feet below the dome's peak. Seen from outside, a nearby exit door is only halfway up the building's exterior wall.

Although the auditorium is immense, it can feel surprisingly intimate. The aisles and seats are wider, with more legroom, than those in other theaters built at the time. Wherever someone sits, the sightlines and acoustics are impeccable. There isn't a bad seat in the house. As architect C.W. Rapp put it, the Uptown "is absolutely the last word in modern building, employing scientific engineering in its acoustics, its placing of seats, its eye-command of screen and stage."

The auditorium is filled with so many fascinating details that no one could take them all in during a single visit, or even dozens of visits. The

The curve of the stairs from the mezzanine to the Grand Lobby floor.

The staircase from the Grand Lobby leads to main men's lounge on the lower level.

Balaban & Katz Magazine told visitors that their spirits would become "gay and light under the spell of the warm coloring that plays across heavily carved and ornamented walls as myriads of unseen lights steal out from mysteriously hidden coves to illumine the interior with romantic sundown colors." Of course, most people turned their eyes to the rococo stage. Rapp & Rapp drew up blueprints for a proscenium 70 feet wide, the same width as the Chicago Theatre stage. According to legend, Balaban & Katz told the architects to add one inch. That enabled B&K to hype the Uptown as the city's widest stage.

As showtime approached, Campbell-Duncan took his seat in the loge, the smallest of the auditorium's many levels, a cozy space with 400 seats. He sat in a "sumptuous, crimson velvet armchair in box E, right in the center of the

The lounge's tile floor. Right: A marble fountain at the crossroads of the theater's three lobbies.

glittering loge horseshoe, beneath the huge balcony that sweeps in a graceful curve 170 feet from wall to wall of the immense auditorium." As he got comfortable, he thought back on the rudimentary nickelodeon movie houses that had been common fifteen years earlier, operated by people such as the Balabans. "It was a nice seat, roomy and deep and soft, with plenty of room for the knees," he remarked. "As I lounged in it, vivid memories were aroused of the days when I used to shift uneasily on a kitchen chair, nailed to its neighbor with a piece of scantling, in a nickelodeon. And that wasn't so very long ago, either."

Looking toward the stage, Campbell-Duncan saw something remarkable: an entire orchestra rising out of the darkness on a sort of elevator, as "iridescent beams from a flood light played over them." The orchestra pit was equipped with a "disappearing stage" that could move up and down 18 feet, rising up when a show began and later vanishing back into the basement. The conductor stood on his own platform, climbing or descending independently from the orchestra's larger elevator. The vision of the Uptown Theatre Orchestra emerging out of the depths reminded Campbell-Duncan of a scene from mythology. "Fewer clothes and some seaweed in their hair and they might have been Neptune and his entourage rising from the sea," he wrote.

Everyone in the theater at the preview that day stood as the orchestra played "The Star-Spangled Banner." The show began with Nathaniel Finston conducting Tchaikovsky's *Capriccio Italien*. The preview was a dress rehearsal for the following day's official opening, so it was occasionally interrupted by the stage manager. "This official,

German Dresden figurines and an Aubusson-style rug decorate the ladies' lounge.

megaphone in hand, popped on and off stage incessantly like the little bird in a cuckoo clock, who shouted orders to the 'flyman' up aloft or the electrician at the vast switchboard backstage," Campbell-Duncan wrote. "All this to the huge delight of the audience."

The music got jazzier, as the Edgewater Beach Hotel's Oriole Orchestra played what Rob Reel called "some fine syncopation specialties." Then everyone watched a newsreel. After that, Jesse Crawford, one of the era's most popular organists, was supposed to play the Uptown's four-manual, eighteen-rank organ, said to be the most expensive Wurlitzer (at $52,500) built at the time. "Its console will raise and lower on elevators," B&K's magazine said. "Ten-thousand pipes ranging in size from the smokestack of an ocean-going liner to a lead-pencil are hidden behind the walls on either side of the proscenium arch. These pipes are made to sound by a highly intricate system of electrical contacts between the organ lofts and the console which the organist plays. This organ is capable of reproducing a symphony orchestra, a military band, a jazz band, a cathedral organ, a choir of feminine or masculine voices, effects of the sublimest beauty or most humorous imitation of the animal kingdom, novelties without limit."

The organ's pipes were hidden behind 65-foot-high grilles flanking the proscenium on both sides—huge metal flowers and vines, framed in richly ornamented and gilt plasterwork, with drapes of burgundy velvet.

But the gigantic instrument was apparently not quite ready on the night of the dress rehearsal. "The mighty Wurlitzer was silent," Reel wrote in the *American*. "A crew of experts had been working night and day to get the great instrument ready, but were unable to accomplish it in time for the dress rehearsal. Those who had precious invitation last night, therefore, had to forgo the pleasure of hearing Jesse Crawford." However, the *Evening Post* published a contradictory report from H. Campbell-Duncan, who described hearing "several selections on the colossal Wurlitzer with Jesse Crawford at the console."

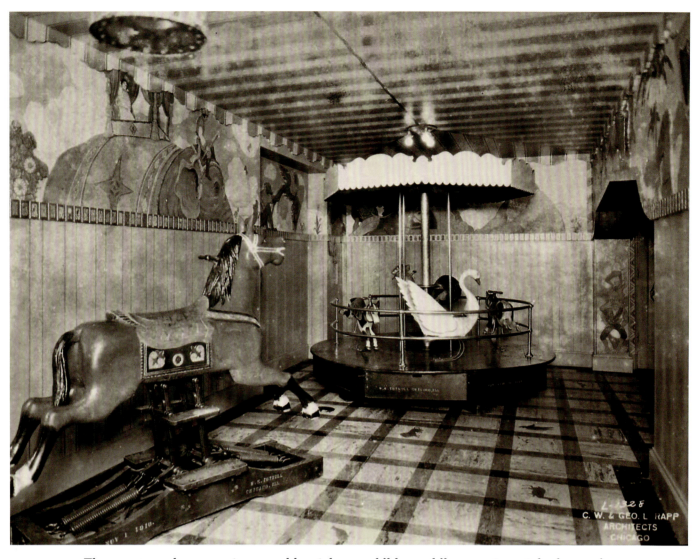

The nursery, where a matron would watch over children while parents watched a movie.

Befitting the Uptown's "Spanish" architectural theme, the opening show also included a performance "flashing with gypsies, habanera dancers, beauties and haughty grandees out of Spain's colorful past." Titled "Under Spanish Skies," it featured tenor Don Jose Mojica, soprano Marie Herron, and Argentine bandleader Juan Carlos Cobián. Reel praised the "truly gorgeous" peacock dance, and also enjoyed the performance by Maria Montero, "a Spanish dancer with color, talent and fire, who shakes her castanets as only one who has learned the art from childhood can."

Harold Green was eyeing how the Uptown's lighting subtly created different moods and atmospheres for each moment during the stage performances. "A tinge of amber to carry out a mellow restful home setting; a smooth but directed flood of greenish-blue light to carry the audience into the moonlight; a brilliant, broken, but ever-directed path of light to give a true effect of shade trees on a summer's day—these are but a few of the ingenious ways in which light lends the actors aid on the Uptown stage." It wasn't surprising that Green paid so much attention to the effects produced by the 17,000 electric light bulbs. He was, after all, a writer for a lamp industry publication. "Light is as much a part of this theater as the very walls that surround it," Green wrote. "Light! They use so much of it here that they need the largest stage switchboard in the world, and just one of their attraction signs takes more current than two entire drama theaters in the Chicago Loop."

After all of the music and stage shows, it was time for the main event—the movie. Despite the Uptown Theatre's enormous size, its screen— revealed when a set of golden gates opened—was

The two rooms that made up the nursery were decorated as a storybook circus.

not especially big. Although the proscenium was 70 feet and 1 inch across, the moving pictures didn't fill all of that space. Instead, they were confined to a smaller rectangle within the proscenium, surrounded by ornate framework and drapery. Photographs from the 1920s indicate that the Uptown's original screen was positioned within a space roughly 43 feet wide—and the screen itself may have been smaller than that due to the limits of the technology at the time.

The feature that week was *The Lady Who Lied,* a star-crossed romance starring Lewis Stone and Nita Naldi involving alcoholism, a safari, a poisonous snake, and caravan-raiding bandits. Like all movies in 1925, it was silent. The orchestra at the Uptown provided a live soundtrack. Afterward, the *Daily News* observed: "The throngs paid more attention to the theater than to the picture." *Tribune* movie critic Mae Tinée (a punny pseudonym used by various writers over the years) commented: "It's a rather long picture. ... Rather TOO long, for there are spaces where it drags interminably. However, graced by good acting and photography, you won't mind it at all and chances are may like it quite a little." One of the film's stars attracted the attention of Rob Reel, who noted that Virginia Valli was "good to look at as the heroine whom it is all about." Valli may have looked familiar to some in the audience. She was "a Chicago girl," Reel wrote, who grew up in Uptown. Her name had been Virginia Helen McSweeney, a daughter of Irish immigrants who started as an extra at Uptown's Essanay movie studio before going to Hollywood. Now, her face was on the big screen in the old neighborhood. After *The Lady Who Lied,* the show concluded with "selected

Patrons walked through the Grand Foyer, also known as the Magnolia Lobby, before entering the auditorium. Following pages: The auditorium, which sat 4,320 people, seen from the balcony level.

comedy," a short that wasn't identified in the program.

Even when movies were being projected, color lights were used for effects in the auditorium. "A silent film with live music could also be accompanied by changing light motifs through the show," Douglas Gomery wrote in his 1992 book *Shared Pleasures: A History of Movie Presentation in the United States*. "In general the lights were kept low, and patrons kept their seats throughout the show. Too much light invited patrons to move about, and that would have become chaotic with full houses of four thousand or more. This was a dignified setting, and patrons responded accordingly."

When the show was over, some audience members exited from the back of the auditorium through French doors onto Magnolia Avenue. Others departed through the auditorium's left side, where they headed south. The corridors in this part of the building converged at the Lawrence Avenue Lobby. Here, they passed a mural depicting parrots flying amid ancient columns. It was one of the murals painted by Louis Grell, who taught a young student named Walt Disney at the Chicago

The auditorium's fanciful organ screen. Left: The orchestra pit beneath the proscenium arch. Following pages: The auditorium's eight levels, from the floor to the projection booth and three-tiered dome.

Academy of Fine Arts. When people emerged from the Uptown Theatre's south end, they found themselves underneath a marquee that extended over the Lawrence Avenue sidewalk.

After the preview on August 17, Rob Reel wrote the whole evening had been "undoubtedly the most pretentious presentation ever offered in a motion picture theater," but spared no praise for the building. "Chicago became the possessor of the largest and finest motion picture theater in the world," Reel wrote. A reporter for *Variety* was also ecstatic about the Uptown's magnificence, writing: "Eclipsing in size, splendor and impressiveness anything that has been built in the last few years of hectic theater construction, this new house is … beyond doubt the most gorgeous movie palace in the world."

Following that preview show, the Uptown Theatre opened at noon on Tuesday, August 18. That wasn't the most convenient time for working

Views from the mezzanine (left) and the balcony.

Chicagoans, but advertisements encouraged people to "cancel all engagements" so they could be there when the Uptown threw open its doors to "an amazed world." More than 12,000 people crowded around the entrance on Broadway. "Never have I witnessed an opening like it," said John Balaban, one of the brothers running Balaban & Katz. "World's championship baseball games I have attended were tame affairs in comparison."

The *Chicago Evening American* described the day's scene: "The Broadway and Lawrence Avenue district looked like a circus yesterday. A veritable standing army gathered before the doors of the magnificent moving picture palace and waited in the hot sun for several hours. They were women for the most part and their gay summer dresses formed a colorful parade, three blocks long. Street vendors sold balloons and refreshments. Within the theater workmen were putting the finishing touches to

57

After the shows, patrons would exit the theater through the two levels of the Lawrence Avenue Lobby.

the carpets, rearranging the vases and pictures for the last time. When the doors were opened the excitement in the street grew more intense, but those who entered the stately lobby filled with flowers became silent and spoke in whispers. Toward the end of the line, several blocks away, the fans became anxious. 'Are the tickets all sold?' they asked anxiously. Even when the house had been filled to its capacity, the crowds still mobbed the streets."

On that Tuesday alone, 200,000 people attended the neighborhood festival, filling Broadway and the surrounding streets, according to the *Daily News*. On Wednesday, a Balaban & Katz ad proclaimed: "All Chicago Stormed the Uptown Theatre. Its opening was the most gigantic thing since Armistice Day—from North Side, South Side, West Side, and far, far up the North Shore, they came and couldn't believe their eyes."

CHAPTER TWO
BACKSTORY

'Uptown Chicago is to me the finest place in all the world.'

Busy Uptown: Clarendon Municipal Beach looking north in the 1910s.

When Balaban & Katz began building the Uptown Theatre in 1924, the surrounding neighborhood was just starting to be called "Uptown." A few decades earlier, it had simply been known as Lake View Township, a rural region north of the Chicago city limits. Conrad Bristle, a German immigrant who moved to the area as a boy in the 1850s, said it often flooded when strong winds blew in from the lake. Everything east of the path that later became Broadway was "sandy timber land," said Bristle, who trapped prairie chickens, quails, and wild pigeons in this sparsely populated realm. As time went on, the area became recognized for its celery farms and cemeteries, as well as the place for the summer homes of Chicago's rich. And it was known for its saloons and roadhouses, which provided drinks and food to those who traveled to its cemeteries. Lake View incorporated as a city in 1887 and was annexed by Chicago two years later.

In 1889, a Chicago saloonkeeper named Charles E. "Pop" Morse bought three vacant lots for $4,420 at the northwest corner of Lawrence Avenue and Evanston Avenue, the street that would later become known as Broadway. It's unclear why Morse decided to buy this property in a remote area six and a half miles north of Chicago's center, that was as the *Inter Ocean* newspaper put it, "little known by the average Chicagoan." Perhaps he had the foresight to predict that the area would boom. The so-called "cemetery saloons," mostly along Clark Street, were certainly an indication of business potential. Whatever his motivation, Morse set in motion a chain of events that would lead to the construction

A view around 1918 looking east toward the Wilson Avenue Theatre, with Broadway in the foreground.

of the Uptown Theatre.

He built a two-story saloon and roadhouse with his wife, Annie, at the corner in 1897. The roadhouse may have attracted visitors from St. Boniface Cemetery, just west of it along Lawrence Avenue, and it became a regular stop for travelers from Chicago to Calvary Catholic Cemetery in Evanston. "Morse conducted a hotel on the 'road to Calvary' and his place was well known to funeral parties," the *Chicago Daily Tribune* stated. "An oft heard saying among mourners was that 'Pop' served the best corned beef and cabbage on the road." None of the old-time politicians passed his place without stopping to have a drink and a bite to eat with the proprietor. Pop's place also contained a boxing ring for fighters to spar. In 1900, the *Inter Ocean* described a group of Brooklyn boxers making a "pilgrimage" to the roadhouse, where they spent the day training. When their trainer had the pugilists run around the area, they marveled at how bucolic the surroundings were. "It's all a park," one said.

Meanwhile, new transportation systems were making it easier for people to reach this spot. In 1900, the Northwestern Elevated Railroad began running trains from Chicago's Loop to Wilson Avenue—just a couple of blocks south of Pop's roadhouse—taking a route that's still used today by CTA lines. The speedy electric trains on the "L" line (which was extended north to Evanston in 1908) sparked a boom in population growth and the rise of a business and entertainment district. The neighborhood soon began attracting thousands of Chicagoans on hot summer days, thanks to its

An advertisement in the *Chicago Tribune* announces Green Mill Gardens' opening on June 26, 1914.

beaches on the Lake Michigan shoreline, including the privately operated Wilson Avenue Bathing Beach and the city-owned Clarendon Municipal Beach.

By the time Morse died in 1908, his wife and nine of his children were no longer living. His estate, including the roadhouse property, was inherited by his one surviving child, twenty-seven-year-old Catherine Hoffman. She leased the roadhouse in 1910 to Tom Chamales, a Greek immigrant already known as a successful saloonkeeper in the Loop. Local residents soon complained that Chamales's roadhouse—as well as the beaches—were attracting "throngs of ruffians," "the criminal element," and "rowdies from less favored neighborhoods in the city." These neighbors wanted their area to stay "as orderly as a country village."

Chamales had different ideas, and so did the other men who owned businesses along Evanston Avenue. They lobbied the city to change the street's name. Reportedly, local saloonkeepers worried that "Evanston Avenue" made people think of Evanston, the dry town just north of Chicago and home of temperance leader Frances Willard. That wasn't the image these business owners wanted for their street. They persuaded city officials to give it a new name—a moniker that evoked New York City's famous theatrical district. At the stroke of midnight on August 14, 1913, Broadway was born.

Chamales demolished the roadhouse and constructed a more lavish entertainment venue in 1914 called Green Mill Gardens, which stretched for a whole block from Broadway west to Magnolia Avenue, encompassing an outdoor area for dancing, dining, and drinking. The *Chicago Daily News* called it "the mecca of those who enjoy music," while noting how the "the dance 'mad' crowd takes to the new outdoor dancing floor."

The neighborhood also happened to be a hub for the fledgling movie industry. At the turn of the twentieth century, many witnessed the miracle of moving pictures, watching plotless short films in amusement parks, traveling shows, nickelodeons, and vaudeville theaters. In the neighborhood that would become Uptown, a movie described as "the Spanish Bull Fight" was shown in 1899 at the Sunnyside Inn on a device advertised as the "Justoscope." The Essanay Film Manufacturing Company opened a studio in 1908 at 1333–45 West Argyle Street, just a few blocks from the corner of Lawrence and Broadway, as movies became a bigger business. Essanay's most famous star was Charlie Chaplin, who arrived in Chicago in 1914. He had made his screen debut less than a year earlier and was fast becoming a movie favorite. But Chaplin didn't stay in Chicago for long. Soon after he filmed the two-reel comedy *His New Job* he left town. The *Los Angeles Times* reported in early 1915 that Chaplin was back in California, where he quipped that Chicago was "too damn cold." Other Essanay actors, including Wallace Beery and Gloria Swanson, also headed to Hollywood. By 1916, Chicago's movie business was in the doldrums. Essanay shut down in 1918.

Ironically, that was the same year that the neighborhood's first movie palaces opened. Across the street from Green Mill Gardens, Chamales had bought up property at the southwest corner of Broadway and Lawrence and built the Riviera Theatre. To design his ambitious project, he hired Rapp & Rapp, a firm led by a pair of brothers who had grown up in the southern Illinois city of Carbondale. The taciturn Cornelius Ward Rapp had been practicing architecture since the 1880s, designing college buildings, courthouses, churches, and municipal structures across Illinois. One of C.W. Rapp's employees called him "that crusty old genius." Another said: "He always looked sore but wasn't."

"To his young designers and draftsman, who saw him once a day at 11 a.m. when he came down the spiral staircase from his office to the drafting room, he was god," his great-nephew Charles Ward Rapp wrote in his 2014 book *Rapp & Rapp: Architects*. "He would pass among the broad drafting tables puffing a pipe as he inspected work in progress. Most often he said nothing. Even with his silence, or maybe because of it, no one doubted his authority."

In 1907, when C.W. was forty-seven, he formed a partnership with his youngest brother, twenty-nine-year-old George Leslie Rapp, who had worked as a draftsman and designer for architect Edmund C. Krause on the towering Majestic vaudeville theater and office building at 18 West Monroe Street. (Known for many years as the Shubert, it is called the CIBC Theatre in 2025.)

The Rapps came from a family of builders. Their father was a building contractor and architect, and their six siblings included another two architects who owned a firm of their own in Colorado.

Cornelius and George named their Chicago firm C.W. & Geo. L. Rapp, Architects. George "occupied Rapp & Rapp's front office," their great-nephew Charles wrote, "where he combined natural charm with his talents as architect, salesman, negotiator, idea man and general liaison between clients and staff alike." In the years ahead, Rapp & Rapp would design many of Chicago's grandest and most famous movie palaces—and many others across the country.

By the time Chamales hired them in 1916, they had designed several movie houses. The first was a modest 1907 nickelodeon at the South Side's Sans Souci Amusement Park. After that, they'd created the Majestic in Dubuque, Iowa (now called the Five Flags Center), and the Orpheum in Racine, Wisconsin.

But Rapp & Rapp didn't fully develop their signature style, inspired by France's Palace of Versailles and the Second Empire style of architecture, until C.W. got married in 1911—to Mary Payne Root, who was twenty years younger than him—and took a long wedding trip to Europe and North Africa. The honeymooners booked tickets on the *Titanic's* fateful maiden voyage in April 1912 but escaped disaster when they postponed their return so they could spend more time on architectural sightseeing at places such as the Palais Garnier opera house in Paris. C.W. "armed himself with a wealth of on-site information about the shape and feel of classic Beaux-Arts treatment and brought home a trunk of books, most notably two large volumes of Charles Garnier's color renderings of Paris Opera detail, and collections of Piranesi studies of classical Rome," his great-nephew wrote.

Back in Chicago, he and George designed movie theaters more elegant and ornate than their earlier creations: the Windsor at 1235 North Clark Street, which opened in 1913; the La Salle Theater at 152 West Division Street; the Orpheum in Champaign and the Orpheum in Quincy, both of which opened in 1914; the Rockford Palace in Rockford, Illinois, and the Al. Ringling Theatre in Baraboo, Wisconsin, both in 1915.

As George Rapp explained in 1925, he wanted to create beautiful spaces that would lift people's spirits, all for the mere price of a movie ticket:

Watch the eyes of a child as it enters the portals of our great theaters and treads the pathway into fairyland. Watch the bright light in the eyes of the tired shopgirl who hurries noiselessly over carpets and sighs with satisfaction as she walks amid furnishings that once delighted the hearts of queens. See the toil-worn father whose dreams have never come true, and look inside his heart as he finds strength and rest within the theater. There you have the answer to why motion picture theatres are so palatial.

Here is a shrine to democracy where there are no privileged patrons. The wealthy rub elbows with the poor—and are better for this contact. Do not wonder, then, at the touches of Italian Renaissance, executed in glazed polychrome terra cotta, or at the lobbies and foyers adorned with replicas of precious masterpieces of another world, or at the imported marble wainscoting or the richly ornamented ceilings with motifs copied from master touches of Germany, France and Italy, or at the carved niches, the cloistered arcades, the depthless mirrors, and the great sweeping staircases. These are not impractical attempts at showing off. These are part of a celestial city—a cavern of many-colored jewels, where iridescent lights and luxurious fittings heighten the expectation of pleasure. It is richness unabashed, but richness with a reason.

As Rapp & Rapp worked for Chamales, they were also drawing plans for Balaban & Katz's Central Park Theatre. The Balaban brothers had grown up on the Near West Side on Jefferson Street, a bustling marketplace in a crowded Jewish enclave that was often called "the ghetto," where their parents, Russian immigrants Israel and Gussie Balaban, ran a food store. After the turn of the twentieth century, the Balabans were among a wave of Russian Jews who moved a few miles west into the North Lawndale neighborhood, with its more

The collaboration of Balaban & Katz and Rapp & Rapp resulted in the Central Park Theatre on the West Side.

spacious streets, yards, and parks. That's where Abraham Joseph Balaban, the second-oldest of the family's eight living children, got his start in show business. A.J.—as he was known—was eighteen years old in 1907, when he was hired to sing at the Kedzie nickelodeon, a storefront with 102 rickety chairs at the corner of Kedzie Avenue and Roosevelt Road (then known as Twelfth Street).

That was the decade when movies became more than a novelty. The exhibition industry was developing, as nickelodeons—theaters that charged five cents—opened around the country starting around 1905. Chicago had a hundred of these little movie houses by 1910. "The nickelodeon functioned as a small and uncomfortable makeshift theater, usually a converted cigar store, pawnshop, restaurant, or skating rink made over to look like a vaudeville theater," movie historian Douglas Gomery wrote. "Inside, the screening of news, documentary, comedy, fantasy, and dramatic shorts lasted about one hour. The show usually began with a song, a hit from the day illustrated with hand-painted, color magic lantern slides displaying the images and words of the song. Most entertainment, though, came from motion pictures."

At the Kedzie, A.J. Balaban was hooked by the audience's response.

"Nothing had ever given me so much satisfaction as to see the happy faces of the audience as they filed out talking about the picture and the illustrated song," he recalled. A.J. persuaded his family to rent the Kedzie for $100 a month and run the shows. Following the advice of A.J.'s older brother Barney, a "genius in finance," everyone in the family helped, which kept expenses low. Barney, who had a job at the Western Cold

Clockwise from upper left: David, Barney and A.J. Balaban, and Sam Katz.

Storage Company, decided the theater needed ventilation, so he installed a huge fan. Managing the nickelodeon gave A.J. an education in how to please audiences. "I found that people liked to be greeted, to be told what the next film would be, and what song I would sing the next day," he said. "After every performance I mingled with the crowd to hear comments—a habit I never lost."

Nickelodeons were so successful that entrepreneurs—including the Balabans—soon built bigger movie theaters. In 1909, they opened the Circle, a 707-seat theater at 3241 West Roosevelt Road. The short movies shown there were just one part of the Balabans' vaudeville shows, which at times featured the Marx Brothers and Sophie Tucker. A.J. believed theaters needed to show a mix of moving pictures and "flesh," as he called the performers. When shows at the Circle received bad reviews, A.J. sought more variety. "Applause wasn't always the best sign to trust," he said, in a 1942 as-told-to memoir authored by his wife, Carrie Balaban. "By making a hole in the wall near the stage I could watch the faces of the people, and those expressions became my guide—not their applause. I felt responsible for making these people happy and gay, to release them even for a moment from the depression of their drab homes and usually burdened lives. That was my big aim, and it dominated my every thought."

A.J. had grander ambitions. He wanted to build 5,000-seat theaters on each side of Chicago—giant "presentation houses" that would host shows combining movies with live entertainment. His friend Sam Katz was skeptical. "It would take too much cash," he said.

Born in Russia, Katz (the K in B&K) had arrived in America when he was just a few months old. Like the Babalans, he'd grown up in the Jewish West Side ghetto. "Every month or two I go down to the ghetto in Chicago and look at the old home and my father's old barbershop at Twelfth and Jefferson Streets," he once told an interviewer. "And it says to me: 'Here's where you came from, Sam Katz. Now be yourself and cut out the applesauce.'" At the age of thirteen, he began a job playing piano in a nickelodeon. Seeing the owner make hundreds of dollars a week, Katz persuaded his father to go into the movie business. "I saw the thing awfully big and went home and said, 'Dad, close up the barbershop. This is a business. This is a real business,'" Katz recalled. By the time he was sixteen, Sam was running a movie theater. But he soon devoted his nights to studying law.

"Sam, someday we will have a picture theater on this street, seating thousands, and it won't only be pictures; we'll have everything," A.J. told Katz one day while walking along State Street in the Loop. Katz and his father eventually formed a partnership with A.J. and Barney. Their families also became intertwined when Sam married A.J.'s sister, Ida Balaban, who would die in 1922.

As they started planning the Central Park Theatre, Barney and A.J. Balaban suggested hiring Rapp & Rapp, whose architecture they had admired for years. "How many hours Barney and I had spent in their offices studying blueprints for theaters we couldn't afford to build!" A.J. recalled. They took the Katzes to Baraboo, showing them the Al. Ringling Theatre.

The Central Park Theatre opened in October 1917 at 3531 West Roosevelt Road with a lavish Spanish Revival design. It was big—1,758 seats—though not nearly as big as the giant theaters A.J. had been dreaming about. But A.J. was pleased with Rapp & Rapp's "spectacular" design of the theater's horseshoe-shaped mezzanine. "It was intended to give the audience the feeling of being part of a stage set," he said. Along with its screen and center stage, the Central Park had two "lunette" side stages, where singers could perform while a silent movie was shown.

The theater's revolutionary central air conditioning system was Barney's idea, inspired by his work for the Western Cold Storage Company. He'd wondered: Could the same technology that cooled food at Western Cold Storage be used to cool off moviegoers? He worked with engineer Frederick Wittenmeier to install carbon dioxide fan-forced air-cooling systems.

As the Central Park opened, A.J. was still dreaming about building bigger theaters. He told a reporter about his vision for the future: 5,000-seat theaters "with artistic themes dedicated to the people and their children's children." He said these theaters would "bring the various arts into one grand finale, blending of the opera to the fastest tempo of jazz" and serving as a "meeting place of the aristocrat and humble worker."

Before construction began on the Central Park Theatre, the *Tribune* reported in 1916 that Rapp & Rapp had completed their design for Tom Chamales's North Side theater, which would be used for vaudeville, "legitimate drama," and motion pictures. Rapp & Rapp designed a structure with ornate details in the French Baroque style, inspired by the Palace of Versailles.

By the time Chamales received a building permit in 1917 for the theater that would become known as the Riviera, he had scaled down his plans. The building, covering a footprint of 150 by 150 feet, would be three stories tall instead of the ten he

CHICAGO ARCHITECTURAL PHOTOGRAPHING COMPANY

Balaban & Katz's Riviera Theatre with original canopy.

had envisioned. Chamales decided to let someone else handle the business of running the theater, leasing it for ten years to Jones, Linick & Schaefer, a company that owned many of downtown's major theaters.

But construction stalled in early 1918 as the cost of building materials increased during World War I. For some reason, Jones, Linick & Schaefer's plans to operate the theater fell through. Lawrence Stern, a banker at S.W. Straus & Company, which held a mortgage on the building, made a telephone call to bring the project back to life. Stern called Balaban & Katz and suggested they should take over the theater. The Straus bankers had worked with B&K arranging a mortgage to finance the Central Park Theatre.

"They were looking for a tenant for an unfinished theater building at Lawrence and Broadway," A.J. Balaban recalled. His older brother wasn't enthusiastic. "Barney told them that we couldn't handle it because we had no available cash, and besides, we wouldn't want it unless it could be finished to our liking," A.J. remembered.

A.J. was skeptical about the building's location. He thought the neighborhood's major crossroads was more than two blocks away, at Wilson and Broadway. And he was worried about the ongoing

Proud "200,000 Chicagoans Kept Cool" last week.

construction of a competing theater nearby, the Pantheon Theatre at 4642 North Sheridan Road, just a few blocks southeast.

The Balabans visited the empty shell of the partially completed theater at Broadway and Lawrence, looking it over with architects Rapp & Rapp. "Much of the original plan as a vaudeville house was impractical for us and would have to be recast," A.J. said. "Nevertheless, I saw in it a dream come true. It was big enough to house long desired features: stage, orchestra pit, fitted playrooms, first aid room in the ladies' lounge, fine dressing rooms for actors, club rooms for orchestra men and ushers, besides a beautiful lobby for comfortable waiting. C.W. Rapp proved by his plans how it could be transformed for our use."

"The name 'Riviera' was chosen for our newest 'fairyland,'" A.J. said. Chamales leased the building to the Riviera Theatre Company, a business run by Balaban & Katz. They found financial backing from three of Chicago's wealthiest business titans: Julius Rosenwald of Sears, Roebuck and Company, taxi king John Hertz, and chewing gum magnate William Wrigley Jr.

"For months I watched the race between the competing Pantheon being built around the corner and the Riviera," Balaban said. "Never shall I forget the time I watched until 4 in the morning, not my own theater but the other one. 'They poured the balcony,' I wailed to my patient wife who had expected me home at 1 o'clock. (I had married the 'one and only' that spring.) She answered, 'Why don't you watch your own house and not the other fellow's?' which I decided was not such bad advice. ... Strikes and regular irregularities had held us up in more ways than one."

In July 1918, advertisements for Balaban & Katz's Central Park Theatre mentioned the Riviera, promising that it would open "soon." But the Pantheon won the race to open first, welcoming moviegoers on September 11, 1918. *Chicago Daily News* movie columnist W.K. Hollander described the Pantheon as "a mammoth house, palatial and costly" and "handsomely decorated." Thousands of people turned out for the opening night of the Sheridan Road theater, which had 3,000 seats, including 2,500 on the main floor.

Hollander noted that movie theaters were continuing to open in Chicago in spite of concerns that the US government's war tax might hurt attendance. A 10 percent tax had been imposed on theater admissions in the fall of 1917. Evening admission for adults was twenty cents at the Pantheon, plus the two-cent war tax.

As crowds filled the Pantheon, construction continued on the Riviera. On October 2, 1918, advertisements announced that the 2,600-seat Riviera, "Chicago's Newest and America's Finest

Theatre," was opening that night. "In All the World No Place Like This," the ads proclaimed. Curiously, the ads did not reveal the title of the motion picture that would be shown. In spite of Balaban & Katz's success, at this time the company did not have access to many of Hollywood's top films, forcing it to show movies passed over by theaters with more influence. But that did not matter on this occasion—the spectacle of seeing the theater itself was enough to lure a huge audience.

"How did the people know that the Riviera was going to be good?" A.J. Balaban asked. "It seems they smell the sweat and the lifeblood that is poured into an idea that serves the public. All day long, boxes, baskets and packages of flowers arrived, telegrams from every part of the country came from friends, old and new, obscure and prominent, congratulating us on a sure success. By 4 o'clock that afternoon the crowds filled the sidewalks extending around the whole block, and when the doors opened at 6, they poured in like a mountain stream tumbling to the valley below. So happily, so possessively they praised everything. They said to each other, 'Isn't it lovely, isn't it grand,' taking pleasure in sharing it as if it was their very own. I recognized many young patrons from the Kedzie, Circle, and Central Park, now with a baby or two. Remarks could be heard on every side, 'Oh, yes, I know the Balabans well. I've always gone to their theatres since their very first one.' Everyone seemed to delight in saying how well and how long they had known us."

One Riviera ad said: "They came from everywhere—from Evanston, Wilmette, Winnetka, Oak Park, Englewood, South Side, West Side and from the immediate vicinity. Many had to wait for hours to get into the theater. Such a crowd never was seen in one place save at the War Exposition and the World's Fair." *Variety* commented: "The theater is magnificent. The decorations are gray and blue, with amber lights giving the necessary warmth of tone."

As it turned out, the opening-night movie was *A Woman of Impulse.* As the silent film showed on screen, S. Leopold Kohls conducted the Riviera Symphony Orchestra—billed as a "synchronizing symphony" and praised by *Variety* as "one of the finest in the country." Writing in the *Daily News,* Hollander asserted: "Of prime importance to Chicago is the launching of the Riviera ... a theater erected for the purpose of presenting the silent drama on a higher scale than anything heretofore seen in this community." Hollander offered just one criticism: "The only regrettable thing is that it is not centrally located in the Loop." But this was, of course, Balaban & Katz's strategy—to open large theaters in outlying parts of Chicago, giving people more options on where to go for entertainment.

A.J. seemed to revel in overhearing people pointing out his family's name on the sign. "One rainy night, I was waiting with an umbrella on the corner of Lawrence and Broadway for my wife, who was coming on the streetcar," he said. "A stranger standing in the same doorway said, 'See that sign up there—Balaban & Katz? I know 'em well. Great guy, that Abe Balaban. He's one of my best friends.' Not recognizing him as anyone I had ever seen before, I hid me and my astonishment under my umbrella."

According to theater historian Douglas Gomery, the Riviera and other B&K theaters continued struggling to obtain the best movies. "Rival circuits had exclusive booking contracts with the major studios," he wrote. "Balaban & Katz took what was left over." This situation was one of the reasons why B&K focused so much on live stage shows. In any case, the Riviera seemed to be a success. "People go to the Riviera because it is the Riviera, and not because Mary Pickford, [Alla] Nazimova, Sessue Hayakawa, Fannie Ward, Dorothy Gish or a score of other stars are there on a particular night," *Exhibitors Herald and Motography* magazine commented in 1919. Barney Balaban insisted that the company never had any trouble finding a "good picture" to show. "Our patrons have confidence in our judgment," he said. "They are convinced that if a picture has particular merit, we will book it."

But in September 1919, just one year after the Riviera opened, *Exhibitors Herald and Motography* reported that Balaban & Katz was making plans

The Uptown Hotel, at the northwest corner of Broadway and Leland Avenue, was built in 1912.

to "build a 5,000-seat house in the Wilson Avenue district to succeed the Riviera, which is to be turned into a vaudeville theater."

The neighborhood around Broadway and Lawrence was commonly known as the Wilson Avenue District in the early 20th century. Loophounds—as the people who frequented downtown saloons were known—called this North Side district "Little Paris."

Businessman Loren Miller started calling it "Up-Town" around 1915, when he opened a department store at 4720 North Broadway, a block south of Lawrence. He saw the store serving his neighbors, especially housewives. "It's plumb foolishness to say that our wives and daughters yearn to travel five or six miles into town to buy dry goods, or even millinery, or coats and dresses," Miller told a nearby businessman. "The female population of this whole North Shore section is in the mood to want what they want when they want it. And I could ask for nothing better than to be the man to give it to them."

Miller started using Up-Town as a description of his store's location. "That particular phrase held a very important trade implication—that up-town was the aristocratic antithesis of down-town," Miller wrote, "and it brought home to every North Shore resident the sensation of making a needless journey down-town." To put it another way, Miller believed the word "uptown" (which eventually lost that hyphen) would remind people that they were some distance from downtown. And they'd think about how much easier it would be to go shopping right in their own neighborhood rather than traveling to the Loop.

"Uptown" started appearing in newspapers in

1921 as a name for the neighborhood. The area's business group officially incorporated at the end of 1923 as the Central Uptown Improvement Association. Soon, advertisements referred to the neighborhood as "Central Uptown," a name that seemed to suggest it was just the central portion of some larger expanse known as Uptown. But when Northwestern University sociology student Harold Charles Hoffsommer wrote a thesis about the area in 1923, he chose to call it the Wilson Avenue District. That's what most local residents called it, according to Hoffsommer. But one longtime resident embraced the "Uptown" moniker. "Uptown Chicago is to me the finest place in all the world," Fred Dale Wood told Hoffsommer. "Within its boundaries is everything for pleasure, comfort, happiness and business activities that can be desired. At its door is one of the world's greatest lakes, a playground of majestic grandeur. ... It is growing so rapidly that one must visit it almost every day to keep pace with it."

Uptown was one of about two dozen commercial centers popping up at major intersections around Chicago's neighborhoods. It soon became Chicago's biggest entertainment district outside of the Loop. People flocked there for fun. "If you seek amusement, Uptown Chicago has long been famed for its unrivaled facilities for pleasure indoors and out," the local business association declared.

A resident of nearby Ravenswood told the *Chicago Daily News* that he preferred the quiet, tree-lined streets of his own neighborhood, but he was glad that "Uptown theaters and beaches are but a step away." An Edgewater resident expressed a similar thought about his own neighborhood's proximity to Uptown: "Bordering the busy uptown district, and yet a decided contrast to it in the matter of noise, Edgewater residents are close to every kind of amusement."

Uptown was dominated by people in their twenties and thirties, most of them renting apartments or living in hotels and boardinghouses. As one Chicagoan observed, the young families "who want home life and children" moved to

Sheridan Trust & Savings at Broadway and Lawrence.

neighborhoods like Albany Park, but "those who want to have 'a good time' go to Wilson Avenue." These were among the reasons why Chicago novelist Edwin Balmer called it "a neighborhood as remarkable as any in America."

Uptown already had a reputation for licentious behavior. The *Northside Sunday Citizen* bemoaned that it was known as "Chicago's world-famed 'Pick Up Paradise.'" The newspaper suggested: "If you would see life as it is lived nowhere else on the face of the earth, build yourself a shack in the Wilson Avenue district." Northwestern's Hoffsommer reported that large numbers of "apparently immoral women" walked the streets, suggesting that many were prostitutes. "It is true that many of these are soliciting trade from the streets," he wrote. But prostitution wasn't the only thing that worried moral conservatives about Uptown: They saw the neighborhood's young people were going out at night and having fun—instead of getting married and starting traditional families. Another sociologist noted that Uptown was Chicago's leading

Uptown nightlife promoted in August 1927.

neighborhood for divorces and spousal desertions.

In a 1921 story for the *Chicago Daily News*, noted journalist Ben Hecht described a woman walking the streets at night in the Wilson Avenue District: "A rouged young flapper, high heeled, short skirted and a jaunty green hat. One of the impudent little swaggering boulevard promenaders who talk like simpletons and dance like Salomes." In Hecht's story, a newspaperman takes this flapper to a neighborhood cabaret. He described the scene inside this unnamed nightclub, offering a glimpse of Uptown's nightlife in the Roaring Twenties:

> *The orchestra filled the place with confetti of sound. Laughter, shouts, a leap of voices, blazing lights, perspiring waiters, faces and hats thrusting vivid stencils through the uncoiling tinsel of tobacco smoke. On the dance floor bodies hugging, toddling, shimmying; faces fastened together; eyes glassy with incongruous ecstasies. ...*
>
> *The orchestra paused. It resumed. The crowd thickened. Shouts, laughter, swaying bodies. A tinkle of glassware, snort of trombones, whang of banjos. ...*
>
> *The din was still mounting. Entertainers fighting against the racket. Music fighting against the racket. Bored men and women finally achieving a bedlam and forgetting themselves in the artifice of confusion. ... The jazz band let out the crash of a new melody. The voices of the crowd rose in an "ah-ah-ah." Waiters were shoving fresh tables into the place, squeezing fresh arrivals around them.*

Uptown's population doubled between 1910 and 1920, reaching nearly 45,000. The neighborhood had an unusually high number of women— 54.1 percent of the population—and a lot of single people. Uptown had far fewer children than most places. And 48 percent of the neighborhood residents were between twenty and thirty-nine years old, compared with 32 percent of the US population. Uptown was also one of the Chicago neighborhoods with the lowest percentage of homeownership: Nine out of ten families rented their apartments or houses. The neighborhood was 99.4 percent white.

Uptown's building boom showed no signs of slowing down. In 1924, the Sheridan Trust and Savings Bank moved into an eight-story terra cotta-clad building towering over the southeast corner of Broadway and Lawrence Avenue. It was one of Chicago's largest office buildings outside the Loop, and boasted of having the city's second-largest bank vault. (Four more floors would be added to the top of the building in 1928.) Across the street, the Loren Miller & Company department store had taken over the bank's former building and was expanding to fill the entire block.

A growing transportation network served the burgeoning population. In 1922, a new set

A 1923 night view of the McJunkin Building, at the southwest corner of Broadway and Wilson Avenue.

of elevated tracks created a faster connection to suburban Evanston. And a new station, opened at Lawrence Avenue in 1923, soon became the hub of 2,500 daily passengers. The Northwestern Elevated Company had been reluctant to build a station at Lawrence, since it was only two blocks from Wilson, but business owners pressured the railroad to add the stop. It handled as many passengers on Sundays as it did on weekdays. "This may be attributed to the unusual amusements found in this part of the city," Hoffsommer wrote.

Commuters and visitors also came to Uptown via streetcars, buses, and automobiles. The conjunction of Sheridan Road, Montrose Avenue, and Broadway was Chicago's third-busiest intersection in 1923, with a daily circulation of 160,000. That included 83,000 automobiles, 31,000 pedestrians, 23,000 bus riders, 22,000 surface car riders, and 2,000 people transferring between modes of transit. The corner of Broadway and Wilson Avenue, a few blocks north, was also busy, but dominated more by pedestrians—42,000 each day. Many of them were heading to movies or concerts or going shopping. "It has been stated that the Wilson Avenue District has a greater number of amusement places than any other like area in the world," Hoffsommer wrote. "In keeping with the number of theaters in the district there is also a large number of food shops, cafes and lunchrooms, not to mention the Chinese chop suey houses and one automat. So rapid are the business changes in this district that it is scarcely possible to keep up with them."

Uptown's theaters attracted people from the neighborhood as well as moviegoers from all around Chicago. As of 1923, the neighborhood's movie houses included the Clark, 4533 North Clark Street, 1,050 seats; De Luxe, 1141 West Wilson Avenue, 1,033 seats; Pantheon, 4642 North Sheridan Road, 3,000 seats; Riviera, 4752 North Broadway, 2,600 seats; and Lakeside, 4730 North Sheridan Road, 998 seats. The Riviera was drawing 40,000 moviegoers each week and selling out some shows. It was also attracting people to see a movie and shop. "It is a well-known fact among businessmen that if they can persuade people to 'window shop' they are well on the way toward getting some for their trade," Hoffsommer observed. "Wilson Avenue merchants have been awake to this, and nowhere in the city will one find more beautifully decorated windows to greet the outgoing crowds from the theater than in the Wilson Avenue District." Local merchants noticed that business dropped off whenever the Riviera was showing an unpopular movie.

CHAPTER THREE

CONSTRUCTION

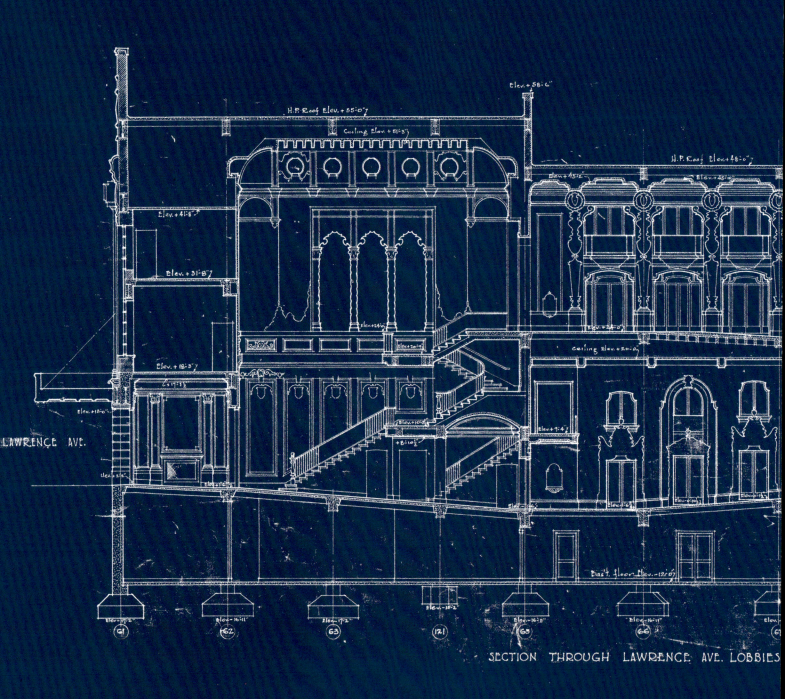

'Full blown magnificence.'

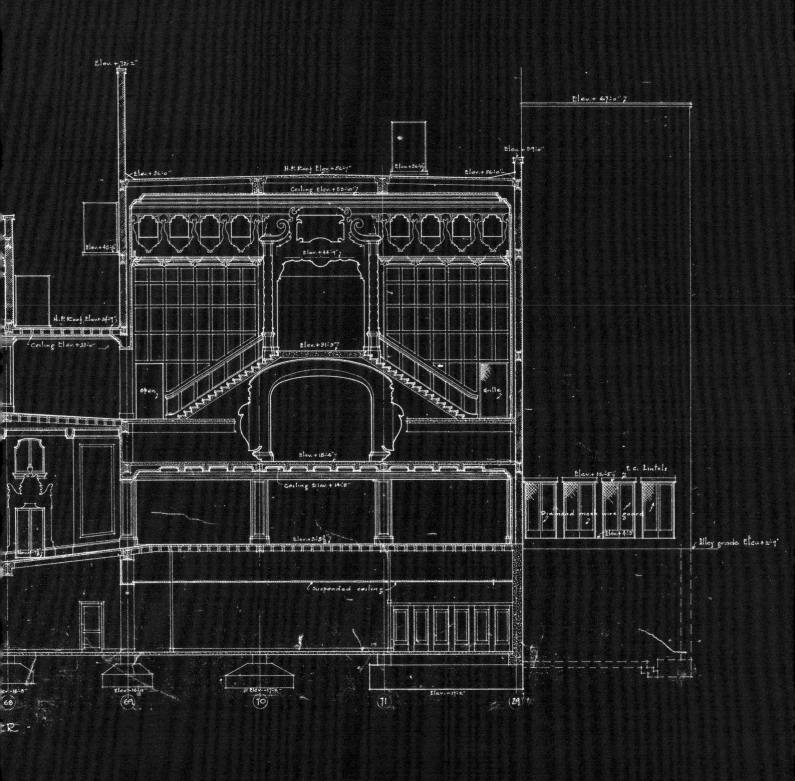

Drawing that shows a cross section of the Lawrence Avenue Lobby and the entrance to the Grand Foyer

The public first learned about Balaban & Katz's ambition to build yet another movie theater in Uptown on May 20, 1923, when the *Chicago Tribune* reported the company planned to build "a gigantic … moving picture playhouse" on land immediately north and west of the Green Mill Gardens building, including that venue's garden area. Early reports said the theater would have 5,600 seats, making it the world's largest cinema.

Several weeks before the *Tribune* article, a vote by the Chicago City Council offered a clue that something was afoot northwest of Broadway and Lawrence. City officials had received a request in March 1923 to vacate one section of a dead-end alley that ran south from Lafayette Street (now called Gunnison Street), ending near the Green Mill Gardens' northwest corner. Otto Annoreno, who shared ownership of the Green Mill Gardens property with Tom Chamales, asked the city to shorten this alley by 75 feet. The Chicago City Council approved Annoreno's request, handing over the land to him in exchange for $3,000. As it happened, Annoreno and Chamales had also just acquired two of the lots along the alley. They seemed to be assembling properties. But nothing had been announced.

Five days after the *Tribune's* report about the movie theater plans, Annoreno and Chamales sold a chunk of the Green Mill Gardens land to Barney Balaban, Sam Katz, and Herbert L. Stern for $400,000. They sold the garden on their building's west side as well as a 10-foot-wide strip of land under the building's north edge. Annoreno and Chamales retained ownership of the rest of the Green Mill Gardens property. But Catherine Hoffman—whose late father, "Pop" Morse, had opened the original roadhouse at this site in 1897—and her husband, Charles, believed they still owned all of the property. The Hoffmans had signed it over to Annoreno, but they insisted that they'd been defrauded. The Hoffmans alleged that Annoreno and Chamales owed them "a very large sum" from this land sale—an accusation never proved in court.

To assemble all of the property for their theater, Balaban & Katz also needed to purchase another five lots immediately north of the Green Mill Gardens property. They bought two of those lots from Annoreno and Chamales. A week later, another property owner sold his two lots. But that left one more lot—at the northwest corner of the theater site, along Magnolia Avenue. It took another eight months before Balaban & Katz succeeded in buying this final piece of the puzzle. In January 1924, Rose I. Davis, a bookkeeper for a law firm representing Balaban & Katz in real estate deals, bought the lot and promptly transferred it to Balaban & Katz. Twelve days after that transaction, demolition and excavation work began. For the time being, the property's owner was called the Broadway Theatre Company. Each of Balaban & Katz's theaters had been a separate business entity until 1923, when they were combined into the Balaban & Katz Corporation. The Uptown property wouldn't be transferred formally to the new corporation until 1926.

Since Balaban & Katz had opened the Riviera Theatre in 1918, the company had built bigger and even more grandiose movie palaces. These fanciful structures seemed like "miracles" to *Chicagoan* magazine movie critic William R. Weaver, who described the businessmen constructing them as "modern necromancers," or magicians. In 1921, Balaban & Katz unveiled two of its crown jewels. The company opened the 3,600-seat Tivoli Theatre in the South Side's Woodlawn neighborhood at Cottage Grove Avenue and 63rd Street, said to be one of the city's busiest intersections. And in the midst of the city's bustling downtown, Balaban & Katz built the 3,880-seat Chicago Theatre at 175 North State Street. Like the Riviera, both of these movie palaces were designed by Rapp & Rapp. These construction projects pushed Balaban & Katz into debt, but Barney Balaban was confident that the Tivoli and the Chicago Theatre would pull in big audiences. "Both theatres are located at points where rapid development in motion picture theater can be expected," he said.

C.W. Rapp saw a logic behind the locations chosen by Balaban & Katz. "They have always selected the sites for theater buildings that will

CHICAGO ARCHITECTURAL PHOTOGRAPHING COMPANY

Two early gems: Balaban & Katz's Chicago and Tivoli theaters both opened in 1921.

be handiest for the public—never the sites that would be cheapest for them," the architect wrote. "They put the theater where the public can reach them in greatest ease." Movie critic Weaver recalled questioning why Balaban & Katz would open yet another theater. Who was going to fill all of those seats? But Weaver noticed how each of these construction projects had a ripple effect: "Community life in its immediate vicinity quickened in anticipation of its opening, new stores springing into life, new values stirring neighborhood trade." And when the theaters opened, they "burst rocket-like in full blown magnificence upon an awed and worshipful public," he wrote. That led Weaver to conclude that Balaban & Katz understood "the psychology of show business" better than anyone else on earth.

Still, it's hard not to share Weaver's initial doubts when considering Balaban & Katz's decision to build the Uptown Theatre. The company was already operating the Riviera, which was just a few years old. And the surrounding neighborhood was saturated with movie houses. In 1924, this part of the North Side had nearly two dozen movie theaters with a total of almost 25,000 seats, giving it the highest theater-seat-to-resident ratio of any Chicago neighborhood outside the Loop. Uptown's theaters reportedly sold $50 million in tickets a year. But movie ticket sales were continuing to rise nationwide. In 1924, Americans bought an average of twenty-one movie tickets over the course of the year. Balaban & Katz's profits and ticket sales were also on the rise. After reporting an operating profit of $1 million for the final six months of 1923, the company made $2.8 million in the first six months of 1925, selling more than 6 million tickets at its five theaters. So, it may not have seemed crazy to construct yet another theater in Uptown, with enough seats to accommodate more than 4,000 people.

By the mid-1920s, small theaters were out of fashion. Barney Balaban argued that it was more efficient to operate mammoth cinemas. "Properly operated moving picture houses having larger theater capacity can be more economically operated," he said. In theory, anyway, it would cost less to run one theater seating 4,000 people than forty theaters

Demolition of the Green Mill Gardens' outdoor space begins for the Uptown Theatre.

CHICAGO ARCHITECTURAL PHOTOGRAPHING COMPANY

with a hundred seats each. "Smaller houses cannot afford to put in conveniences for patrons that larger houses can," said Ernest Lieberman, a structural engineer who worked on the Uptown Theatre. "A four thousand-seat house at this time could have all improvements now known in the industry." *Motion Picture News* magazine made a similar point, arguing that theaters needed to be large so that they'd be "capable of accommodating a sufficiently large number to pay the enormous overhead on an elaborate program as well as a huge property investment." Frank Cambria, Balaban & Katz's art director, asserted that the size of such theaters was an attraction in itself—most people liked to follow the crowd, he explained, so they would flock to a giant theater to join the throngs.

As Balaban & Katz embarked on this project with Rapp & Rapp, the movie theater company and the architectural firm had offices across the street from each other in the Loop. Balaban & Katz was in the Chicago Theatre, while Rapp & Rapp worked on the top floor of the State-Lake Building, which they'd designed in 1919. Barney Balaban spent many hours huddled over the drafting table of C.W. Rapp, according to C.W.'s great-nephew Charles Ward Rapp in the book *Rapp & Rapp: Architects*. The book describes Barney Balaban and C.W. Rapp's working relationship: "Together, they faced the endless problems of creating new temples of entertainment, and since Balaban was in debt anyway, cost ceased to be an object. The imaginative Balaban sometimes got ahead of himself, and Rapp would say something like: If you're the architect you don't need me. At such moments, Balaban backed away, but frequently he sought another authority by pulling aside any workman on the job to ask if he liked a certain treatment. If not, Balaban was known to order the offending portion torn out. To him the common man was the potential customer who knew best."

Work started on the Uptown Theatre site on February 4, 1924, as the garden area west of the Green Mill Gardens building was cleared. Ten feet were sliced off the Green Mill Gardens building's

CHICAGO ARCHITECTURAL PHOTOGRAPHING COMPANY

Excavating space for the Grand Lobby. The Green Mill building is to the left.

north end to make room for the construction work. The city issued a building permit in May, and later that month, pile-drivers were at work. The theater's steel framework took shape in June. The roof's beams were riveted in October. All of the steel was in place by the end of November. Paschen Brothers, one of the city's largest construction companies, which had started as a tuckpointing business in 1871, the year of the Great Chicago Fire, was the lead contractor.

Balaban & Katz spent more than $4 million constructing the Uptown Theatre. The firm spared no expense when building their movie palaces. That was obvious to anyone examining all of the ornaments and decor. But it was also true of the structure, said C.W. Rapp, explaining that Balaban & Katz used one-third more steel than necessary to make sure their theaters were structurally sound. Rapp said the movie palace impresarios showed a "prodigality of precaution and sincerity of purpose," sinking heavy steel posts extra deep into the bedrock and putting two steel posts in places where only one was needed. All of this extra effort "strengthens and strengthens a house until it becomes certain that hundreds of years must pass before Time will notice it," Rapp stated.

Balaban & Katz's representatives bought loads of marble, bronzes, and oil paintings in Europe. Marshall Field & Company supplied antique and reproduction accoutrements worth $23,000. The Uptown was packed with so many furnishings that Balaban & Katz later moved some of them to the

Michigan Theatre when that movie palace opened in Detroit in 1926.

"They really didn't need to spend the kind of money they did," said Joe DuciBella, a movie theater historian who worked at the Uptown during his youth in the 1960s. "They didn't need to design custom plaster designs. They could have pulled things out of catalogs. But they figured, 'Oh well, we've got the money. We've got the time.' … It's very much a custom design."

"The Uptown came along at the crest of a frivolous wave," Donald K. Lampert and Leonard D. Williams wrote in a 1986 report nominating the Uptown for the National Register of Historic Places. "Attesting to the 'no expense spared' budget are such fine features as solid cast bronze railings and radiator grills in place of the standard iron; marble baseboards and door surrounds; use of real gold leaf; the custom carpet whose heraldic shields were reproduced in the railings and stained glass; cast bronze custom lighting fixtures that were plated in twenty-two-carat gold, and the list could go on. … The Uptown was, and is, a testament to all that was the 1920s in America; an era of unbounded prosperity, youthful ideals, passion, fantasy, and escapism."

Rapp & Rapp designed the Uptown to resemble an idealized Spanish Renaissance castle. Spanish Colonial Revival architecture was popular at the time, especially in California and Florida, inspired in part by the building designs at the Panama-California Exposition of 1915 in San Diego. Another spark for the fad may have been *The Mark of Zorro,* a hit 1920 movie starring Douglas Fairbanks as the daring swordsman in a black mask and cape. The 1920s were the heyday of those Hollywood sex symbols known as "Latin Lovers," typified by Italian actor Rudolph Valentino (whose character in 1922's *Moran of the Lady Letty* was Spanish) and Mexican actor Ramon Novarro. While Spanish architecture never became nearly as popular in Chicago, the style could be seen in a few of the city's major structures. "The Spain of bygone years lives in every feature of the Uptown," *Good Furniture & Decoration* magazine commented.

"Crimson velours stretch upward in panels that are copied from originals in Seville, the giant pillars that rise in deep and heavy carvings are from models in Madrid; even the great and intricate chandeliers that sparkle in the lobbies are copies of Hidalgo craftsmanship."

The Spanish theme gave Balaban & Katz's copywriters a chance to use an old expression. "Old people say to starry-eyed dreaming young people 'Stop building castles in Spain,'" they wrote. "By that they mean that rosy, romantic and beautiful plans of youth never come true. But here is the Uptown Theatre. It is beyond human dreams of loveliness, rising in mountainous splendor, achieving that overpowering sense of tremendous size and exquisite beauty—a thing that comes miraculously seldom. It is more imaginative and dream-like than anybody's Spanish castles and yet it is one of the most practical, common-sense structures, one of the most downright comfortable places in the world. It took millions of dollars and almost a year of work by builders and artists to make it so, but it is worth all that, for it means enchantment—the one thing we all crave no matter what we name it, entertainment, 'a show,' romance or—enchantment."

Although Spanish architecture was the main inspiration for Rapp & Rapp, the Uptown's details draw on other styles, including heraldic, Tudor, French Baroque, Byzantine, and Islamic. After H. Campbell-Duncan walked through the Uptown in 1925, he remarked: "The architects, I am told, refer to the style of the building as 'Spanish Mexican renaissance.' I've no doubt they are right." The Uptown and other movie palaces certainly weren't faithful reproductions of the Europeans castles and cathedrals they evoked. "These were large, rich-looking buildings with details that didn't mean anything taken out of context from the periods of classicism and neoclassicism and assembled into one hodgepodge," architect Karl Hartnack observed in a 1969 *Tribune* article looking back at the heyday of movie palaces. But while the theaters were pretentious, they were also "a hell of a lot of fun," Hartnack said.

Author Ben Hall celebrated the neo-Baroque

CHICAGO ARCHITECTURAL PHOTOGRAPHING COMPANY

Looking northeast from Magnolia and Lawrence Avenues, workers can be seen atop the truss.

architecture of Rapp & Rapp in his 1961 book *The Best Remaining Seats*, but with a gently mocking tone. "Rapp & Rapp put one idea above all others: eye-bugging opulence," Hall wrote. "They knew (just as the others did) what the public wanted in its movie palaces, but their theaters offered escape not into a world of starlit gardens or double damask dignity or temples of Vishnu; their stock in trade was a grandeur that spelled m*o*n*e*y to the dazzled two-bit ticket holder." In *New York Times* film critic Bosley Crowther's introduction to Hall's book, he counseled: "Let us not be too hoity-toity with our judgments. ... The intent of the temple builders and the wizards who elaborately conceived the stage shows and other bold attractions that adorned these theatres, was not to please ... serious critics of American art. It was to attract the susceptible mass audience and to delight it with extreme, eye-filling shows. ... We are a people who go for—and have gone for—the gaudy and bizarre."

But even during the golden age of movie palaces, some naysayers criticized the buildings. In a 1927 essay for *American Mercury* magazine, W.A.S. Douglas bemoaned the "gaudy horror" of Chicago's movie palaces, adding that they "stink with class." In spite of such scoffing, millions loved movie palaces. "All Balaban & Katz theaters spelled opulence to the average Chicago moviegoer," Douglas Gomery wrote. "It was a special treat to go to these theaters." Wrote Ben Hall, "it was the movie palace that really put Chicago on the entertainment map in the Twenties."

And it wasn't just Chicagoans who worshipped weekly at these temples of entertainment. "Movie

CHICAGO ARCHITECTURAL PHOTOGRAPHING COMPANY

The steel frame of the Lawrence Avenue Lobby and the first section of the stagehouse is erected.

palaces sprang up in vast and shining numbers across the land; their towering electric signs … were beacons in the darkness over a thousand Main Streets," Hall wrote. "They spelled out fun, enchantment, and escape to all the millions in the Twenties who wanted so desperately to believe in make-believe." Wrote Maggie Valentine in her 1994 book *The Show Starts on the Sidewalk:* "Movies, by their very nature, are artificial and impossible. They demand illusion on the part of the viewer. The audience wants to be fooled and tricked and entertained. … The old movie theaters addressed this need for illusion."

Frank Cambria, the art director who planned the decorative schemes for the Tivoli, Chicago, and Uptown theaters, rejected criticisms that Balaban & Katz's palaces were too flamboyant. He insisted that "colors and styles of a florid nature" were necessary in big theaters because they were "catering to a large number of people and therefore representing the majority opinion of what is attractive." To make a good first impression on people in search of amusement, theaters needed to create a sense of brightness and gaiety, using "spaciousness, elegance, and the vivid coloring of a fairyland," he said. "Details are needed to add definite points of impression. These become 'talking points' or reminders which serve to make conversation in which visitors describe the theater to others and thus carry forward the mouth-to-mouth publicity."

Balaban & Katz also believed that lavish decorations gave large buildings a feeling of intimacy, as a company representative explained to *Good Furniture & Decoration* magazine: "It

Electricians pose with decorative lighting on the auditorium floor during construction.

must have the skill of decorators to give a sense of closeness and warmth to the auditorium. For no matter how scientifically this acre of seats may be placed, the holders will feel lost unless there is an overtone of comfort, ease and intimacy about the entire interior."

The company argued that it was elevating American culture—not just showcasing the art of movies, music, and theater—and shaping the way people behaved. "Entering a magnificent theater such as this, almost anybody will be upon his good behavior," B&K's rep told the magazine.

"He will comport himself with propriety and in full consideration of his neighbor's rights. Majestic architecture and rich furnishings have a refining effect no matter where they may be employed. Go into a wonderful church or cathedral and immediately you become reverent regardless of the presence or absence of religious feeling. The architecture—the interior decorating scheme, if you want to put it that way—influences and awes you."

Rapp & Rapp and Balaban & Katz brought their architectural signature feature, a balcony spanning the auditorium's entire width without

I. WALLENSTEIN PHOTO

any columns blocking first-floor views of the stage, to the Uptown. They had built such galleries at the Tivoli and Chicago theaters, but not without controversy. When the Tivoli opened in 1921, some questioned whether the 1,400-seat balcony was strong enough to hold the oversize crowd ("a mob completely out of control," A.J. Balaban recalled) that pushed into the theater on opening night. "Many looked up in fear at the huge balcony filled with people, and said, 'What if it fell!'" Balaban wrote. "This spread to an ugly rumor that it would fall, which persisted for many months after, until we made a cement test that established the indisputable fact that it was safe."

The cement test was likely similar to the demonstration Balaban & Katz performed at the Chicago Theatre, where the cantilevered balcony was loaded with sandbags to prove its strength. People who'd never seen such wide balconies without columns holding them up may have thought they were defying the laws of physics, but the structures actually just made smart use of truss cantilevers and a steel-and-concrete cross beam.

A similar stunt was publicized at the

Uptown—but this time, bags of cement weighing 120,000 pounds were piled on the floor of the lobby, demonstrating the structure's "Super-Safety." The Uptown's balcony spans across an auditorium 170 feet wide and 213 feet deep, with a ceiling about 100 feet above the main floor. The 1,623-seat balcony is so large that it has four cross aisles running across its width.

The Uptown Theatre also has a deeper stage than B&K's earlier theaters, with 36 feet of working space behind the movie screen, "giving room for the staging of the most gigantic spectacles." A.J. Mayger, an architect who worked with Rapp & Rapp, explained: "A deeper stage, as in the Uptown Theatre, permits greater flexibility of performance, and is necessary in order to have presentations along with pictures."

"Motion picture theaters generally were being built with platforms only or stages of very small proportions, never thinking that eventually a tremendous sized and important production would have to be part of a motion picture theater program," Cambria wrote. "Up to recently this method was practiced until Balaban and Katz in Chicago had foresight enough to see that the larger theater with a larger seating capacity and a larger stage, upon which could be produced anything from grand opera to a grand musical revue, would be the only theater to keep pace with the times."

The designers said they didn't cram as many seats in as possible, choosing instead to give audience members more space and comfort. "Better to seat fewer people than to give any patrons discomfort in crowding through aisles or lobbies or exits," C.W. Rapp wrote. "And yet the Uptown has as many seats as the tremendous Chicago Theatre. It has an acre of seats, and all of them *good* seats. The number is deceptive, for each seat seems so close to the stage and screen and orchestra that it seems impossible that there should be approximately 5,000 of them."

How would so many people get in and out of the Uptown Theatre? Whenever Rapp & Rapp designed theaters for Balaban & Katz, they ensured that the buildings had more than enough exits.

"Every house we have erected for them has an excess of exits over and above all requirements," C.W. Rapp wrote. In Rapp's essay, he didn't mention Chicago's Iroquois Theatre, where 602 people died in a 1903 fire as they struggled to get out. But that was surely on his mind as he designed his theaters. If a fire ever broke out in the Uptown Theatre, a steel fire curtain weighing fifty tons with a counterweight of forty-five tons would be dropped behind the proscenium. It was raised and lowered by a hydraulic system that would work even if the building lost electrical power.

The air conditioning may have been the most popular feature of Balaban & Katz's theaters. The mechanics of movie theaters had gone through a revolution over the previous decade, Barney Balaban said, including improvements in ventilation, air washing, and air refrigeration. "The underground system of cooling, involving the introduction of cold air through the floor of theatres, has not proved practicable," Balaban said. "The overhead system now being installed in new houses is more satisfactory."

According to the *Balaban & Katz Magazine* special issue promoting the Uptown Theatre, "The largest and most complete freezing and air-washing plant in the world is in use deep down under the theater."

"Do you know of anything more wonderful or marvelous than the system of air cooling in the Uptown Theatre?" asked an advertisement for Chicago's Brunswick-Kroeschell Company, which supplied air conditioning equipment to Balaban & Katz. "Isn't it great to be able to attend this theater and be perfectly cool and comfortable throughout the entire performance no matter how sticky and hot it may be outside? The air in this theater is as pure, healthful and refreshing as the mountain breeze. The Brunswick-Kroeschell ice machines that cool the air in this theater have a capacity equal to the melting of 365 tons of ice per day. Figure it out on the basis of what you are paying for ice at so much per hundred and you will be astonished when you realize what progressive theater owners, like Balaban & Katz, are spending to make the patrons

CHICAGO ARCHITECTURAL PHOTOGRAPHING COMPANY

Three tiers of the dome are suspended in the attic, with access to change light bulbs.

of their theatres comfortable."

As costly as it was to provide AC, Barney Balaban saw it as a source of revenue. "Air washing and refrigeration enables houses to be operated at a profit in the summertime," he said. In hot weather, the Uptown sometimes allowed air-conditioned drafts to escape through its front doors, enticing passersby.

Although America was entering the age of the automobile, Balaban & Katz did not include a parking lot or garage when they planned the Uptown. Clearly, they expected most of their patrons to arrive by train, streetcar, or on foot. In 1925 and 1926, the Chicago City Council banned parking on Broadway and Lawrence near the theater, as the city installed traffic lights and streetlights on Broadway.

As three-quarters of a million people flocked to the neighborhood during the week of the Uptown Theatre's opening in August 1925, many capped off their evenings by dancing, dining, and drinking at the Rainbo Gardens nightclub over at Clark Street and Lawrence Avenue. The Montmartre Cafe, which had taken over the former Green Mill Gardens space practically next door to the Uptown, must have had big audiences as well. Another Uptown hot spot, Paddy Harmon's Arcadia Hall on Broadway near Montrose Avenue, hosted a "celebrities ball" that Friday, where "movie, radio, stage and baseball stars" appeared among the celebrants.

The week's hoopla boosted business at Uptown's shops. As one report noted, the new theater was "situated in the midst of millinery, ready-to-wear and shoe shops, as well as a good sprinkling of men's shops." A *Variety* reporter seemed unimpressed with the neighborhood, remarking that the Uptown Theatre "is so far above its neighborhood that the North Side will be years

An Uptown seat end panel (bottom left) and examples of its pink-cased glass ceiling lights and sconces.

ERIC J. NORDSTROM PHOTOS

before it is worthy of it." However, the reporter also remarked: "It is a monument to the North Side and a gold feather in the caps of the B&K organization. The appearance of the house will undoubtedly draw all the picture fans from the North Side and will even steal some from other sections of the city." A *Chicago Evening Post* editorial said the Uptown neighborhood was an example of emerging new business districts. "These new Chicagos are in appearance cities in themselves, and they have all those things which make for business, pleasure, social intercourse and for a better and greater Chicago generally," the newspaper said, as it praised the "imposingly beautiful new theater."

During its first six days of operation, the new theater pulled in more than $37,000 in box office receipts, *Variety* reported. The Uptown seemed to be hurting attendance at theaters in the Loop, although people were still waiting in long lines to see Charlie Chaplin in *The Gold Rush* at downtown's Orpheum. Balaban & Katz signed a deal turning over the Riviera Theatre's operations to the Orpheum Circuit, with B&K taking a share of profits. The *Balaban & Katz Magazine* insisted that the Riviera "is not to be overshadowed by the Uptown," explaining: "It will house vaudeville of the very best kind, the very acts that are shown at the Palace Theatre in the Loop will move out to it and the best motion pictures will be shown there, too. The Uptown is to show different kind of programs. The two houses won't conflict." But it was soon reported that the Uptown was taking business away from the Riviera.

As the Uptown opened, three groups of musicians and entertainers rotated to Balaban & Katz's big theaters in the city: the Chicago, Tivoli, and Uptown. "Fresh ideas, fresh talent, fresh originality will be supplied each week by this method," the *Balaban & Katz Magazine* said. In any given week, the audience at one of these theaters might see an orchestra conducted by Nathaniel Finston, H. Leopold Spitalny, or Adolph Dumont. And they would hear Jesse Crawford, Milton Charles, or Albert Hay Malotte at the organ. "All of these artists have huge personal followings in the theatres where they have been playing," B&K's magazine said.

Balaban & Katz vowed to show only the best movies available at the Uptown. Its experts were "viewing and reviewing the motion pictures that the studios send forth, choosing some, discarding others, hunting for those best suited to the enormous army of Chicagoans who depend upon Balaban & Katz for their entertainment." That may have been mostly hype, but the company was indeed gaining new power in the movie industry. In the months after the Uptown Theatre opened, Balaban & Katz teamed up with Hollywood's largest studio, Famous Players-Lasky, which made movies under the Paramount banner. Together, the companies created a national chain in late 1925 called Publix Theatres. This gave B&K the first choice of all the best movies and entertainers, the company said in an advertisement, making the point with italics: *"We are the logical first market for every producing genius, so that our theaters have the choice of everything worthwhile. BALABAN & KATZ THEATRES WILL CONTINUE TO BE THE DESPAIR OF ALL IMITATORS."*

When the Uptown Theatre opened in 1925, C.W. Rapp said it was the "crowning glory" of the movie palaces Balaban & Katz had built. He was also suggesting that the Uptown was one of Rapp & Rapp's greatest achievements. Rapp held out the possibility that Balaban & Katz might top themselves again. "What they do in the future may uncover further progress," he wrote. "That remains to be seen."

Rapp & Rapp soon designed another extraordinary movie palace for Balaban & Katz, the Oriental Theatre, which opened in 1926 at 24 West Randolph Street in the Loop. As the name suggests, the Rapp brothers and their designers looked this time to the East for exotic elements rather than evoking the elegance of old Europe. The building's "hasheesh-dream decor," as Ben Hall called it, drew heavily on India for inspiration, with elephant-throne chairs, Hindu gods, and Buddhas. "No maharaja ever saw anything like the Oriental," the

Daily News marveled. But C.W. Rapp did not live long enough to design any more movie palaces for B&K. He died of a stroke on June 28, 1926, leaving younger brother George to carry on.

Just twelve days after the Uptown Theatre opened amid a burst of hoopla in August 1925, the city issued a building permit for a dance hall down the street. Before construction began, it was already being hyped as "the largest and most beautiful ballroom in the world." It would be called the Aragon Ballroom and would rank as another one of Uptown's major entertainment venues. The owners were Andrew and William Karzas, Greek immigrants who had made a name when they opened the majestic Trianon Ballroom in 1922. That dance hall, at 62nd Street and Cottage Grove Avenue on the South Side, set a high standard for ballroom dancing in luxurious surroundings.

The Karzas brothers opened the Aragon in July 1926 at the northwest corner of Lawrence and Winthrop Avenues—roughly one block east of the Uptown Theatre. A major movie palace architect, Austrian-born John Eberson, created the breathtaking interior space, which looked like a courtyard in Spain at night. Eberson believed in creating "atmospheric" spaces. As he explained, he would create "a magnificent amphitheater under a glorious moonlit sky ... an Italian garden, a Persian court, a Spanish patio, or a mystic Egyptian temple-yard ... where friendly stars twinkled, and wisps of cloud drifted."

The Aragon and the Uptown both offered Chicagoans an illusion: the promise that they could step from the city's sidewalks into a space from medieval Spain. "The spell of old Spain!" an ad for the Aragon proclaimed. "As expressed in exquisite Aragon, it assumes a magic power, transforming the modern girl into a flashing Carmencita—surrounding her escort with the glamour of a Castilian cavalier. Drab reality is banished as entranced couples dance in this enchanting atmosphere." The Spanish theme even extended to the Aragon's employees: "A dark skinned caballero in wide brimmed hat and polished patent leather boots greets the guests as they enter," the *Daily Northwestern* reported.

If any question remained about what to call the neighborhood around the Uptown Theatre, the theater's giant illuminated signs spelling out the word "UPTOWN" declared the obvious answer. The movie palace's looming presence and its renown surely helped determine what people called the neighborhood. In 1927, the Northside Citizen Publishing Company, which published weekly newspapers, started a new edition called the *Uptown Citizen*. That same year, the Central Uptown Chicago Association ran an advertising campaign touting the neighborhood as a city unto itself. It was just one neighborhood within the far larger city of Chicago. But if you lived in "The City called Uptown Chicago," you had everything you needed. "Nothing is lacking in Uptown Chicago," one ad said. "Nowhere else will you find a community quite as complete as Uptown Chicago. One could live quite satisfactorily within its borders and never step beyond them. Though but a section of a city, it has in itself every accessory of a city—delightful places in which to live, dozens of smart and utilitarian shops, great churches and strong banks, and every imaginable form of entertainment. Life is lived at its best in Uptown Chicago."

This campaign said the neighborhood was the "Shopping Center of a Million People." And while Uptown was accessible by elevated trains and streetcars, business ads emphasized the neighborhood's ample parking. "There's parking space for your car, wide sidewalks to walk upon without being elbowed or jostled, frequent and speedy transportation if you'd rather not shop from your car, and cheerful courtesy wherever you go. And, of course, some of Chicago's finest restaurants and dining rooms if hunger assails you while you shop."

The association seemed to think that Uptown could just keep on growing: "Uptown Chicago wants more of both—more folks to live in its famed apartments, more visitors to enjoy its metropolitan life. It is the greatest of the many cities within the city of Chicago—come and learn why."

A worker stands near the top of the monumental terra cotta facade as construction nears completion.

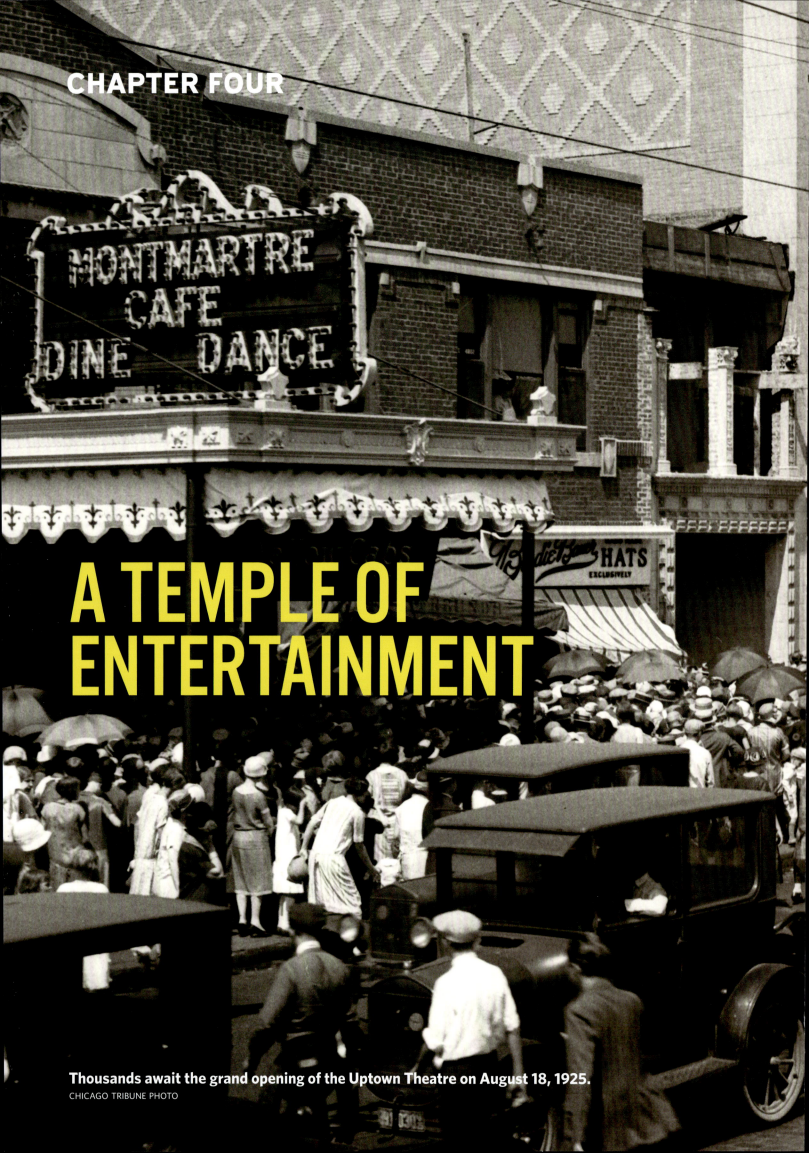

CHAPTER FOUR

A TEMPLE OF ENTERTAINMENT

Thousands await the grand opening of the Uptown Theatre on August 18, 1925.
CHICAGO TRIBUNE PHOTO

N ACRE OF SEATS
N A MAGIC CITY

WELCOME - TO BALABAN & KATZ UPTOWN THEATRE - WELCOME
ONE OF THE GREAT ART BUILDINGS OF THE WORLD - AN ACRE OF SEATS

'Every man was king.'

When people walked up to the Uptown Theatre to see a show, they often didn't know when the feature movie would begin. In the 1920s, newspaper ads for theaters rarely included specific information about the schedules for movie showings. For instance, the Uptown's ad on February 1, 1926, announced that theater was showing *We Moderns,* starring Colleen Moore. But it didn't say when the movie would appear on the screen. The only times mentioned were 1 p.m., when the "tea matinee" began, and 5:30 p.m., the cutoff time for cheaper matinee prices.

Under A.J. Balaban's philosophy of "continuous performance," people could show up at a theater any time after the doors opened. If seats were open, they might sit down in the middle of that day's variety show. Or they might spend some time in the luxurious lobbies until audience members exited from the show in progress. If they wanted, people could stay all day and all night. If patrons entered during a performance and tried to go down an aisle, the ushers would say, "Would you mind waiting until the musical number is concluded?"

It was apparently common for people to ask how long they'd have to wait to get a seat. A Balaban & Katz employee manual told cashiers how to respond: "Never inform patrons as to length of wait. In such cases, refer them to the doorman in the following manner—'Would you kindly ask one of the doormen? He is better informed than I am.'" If any patrons asked whether the show was good, employees were instructed to say: "The comments are good, sir. I am sure you will enjoy it." A Balaban & Katz document reveals the Uptown Theatre's precisely timed schedule for entertainment during that first week of February 1926: Over one day, the Uptown showed *We Moderns* five times: at 2:00, 4:20, 5:54, 8:15, and 10:35 p.m.

As patrons showed up outside the Uptown, some surely picked up snacks at nearby shops. Like other movie theaters in that era, the Uptown did not have concession stands initially. Snacks were sold at a few entertainment events—it was

USHER   FLOOR MANAGER   CHIEF USHER

a common practice at carnivals and burlesque shows—but it was considered low-class at movie palaces. However, Uptown's moviegoers with a sweet tooth had plenty of options: Two Canevin's Candies shops were hyped as "The Sweetest Place in the Uptown District." Over at the southeast corner of Lawrence and Broadway, a Martha Washington Candies shop was in the towering new Sheridan Trust and Savings Bank building—just one of three Martha Washington stores in the neighborhood. Northwest of the same intersection, a drugstore with a soda fountain was in the Green Mill Gardens building. Vaudevillian Rudy Horn, whose father ran the Montmartre Cafe in the same building, thought of that drugstore as "the candy store on the corner." And a Fannie May store opened in November 1925 in a new building Rapp & Rapp designed at 4812 North Broadway, sandwiched between the Uptown Theatre and the Green Mill Gardens building.

A select group of patrons arrived by automobile, pulling up in front of the theater on Broadway. On Saturday nights, this was where passengers wearing jewelry stepped out of chauffeured limousines. The footmen who greeted

| ELEVATOR OPERATOR | PAGE BOY | DOORMAN | STREETMAN | FOOTMAN |

Period examples of Balaban & Katz theater employees and their uniforms. Most wore gloves.

them held one of the few jobs for which Balaban & Katz recommended hiring African Americans. The company advised theater managers: "Your footman should be a colored man, about 6 feet in height, medium heavy, erect, about fifty years of age, preferably with some gray hair, approaching the old southern coachman type; one who thoroughly appreciates, and through previous training has learned the rudiments of courteous service."

Footmen—who always wore classic white gloves unless extremely cold weather forced them to slip on leather—told chauffeurs and other motorists where they weren't allowed to park around the theater on Broadway. "When a cab or automobile draws up at your theater entrance, bow politely, salute by touching the visor of your cap and then open the door," the employee instruction manual said. "The idea of this is to extend a feeling of welcome. Do not touch patrons in assisting them out of or into automobiles except where assistance is plainly desired, such as in the case of incapacitated persons, elderly persons or ladies carrying small children, and then only after saying, 'May I assist you, ma'am?' … Always look directly at the person to whom you are talking. It makes your statements more easily understood and lends an element of refinement to your service."

Like other employees, footmen were warned not to engage in flirtatious conduct, including "looking them over." And the company commanded footmen, as well as other employees, to accept no tips. "You will experience occasions when some patrons are so persistent in forcing upon you a gratuity that they will throw money upon the ground as they leave in their cars," the company said. "In this case you will call one of the management immediately and turn the tip over to him."

Balaban & Katz wanted a particular sort of person to fill each job—specifications that would break discrimination laws if an employer followed them today. For example, the doormen who took people's tickets were supposed to be "men about fifty years of age, who are well preserved, rather tall with a bit of gray hair." As the company explained, "This type of man is capable of transmitting by his appearance the atmosphere which you should be striving to build up throughout your theater." The company recommended hiring African Americans as footmen, porters, maids ("colored girls about twenty-five or thirty years of age, well past the frivolous and playful age, of a serious and quiet nature, of medium stature"), and service boys and messengers ("the smaller type of negro boy, not over 5 feet 4, of slight or slender build ... not markedly of the negro type with heavy features"). Meanwhile, the Uptown Theatre placed a classified ad seeking "directorettes," a job for brunette girls over seventeen years old who were the "tall Spanish type." Balaban & Katz acted as if it were casting actors for a movie.

Whenever crowds gathered outside the theater to buy tickets, Balaban & Katz's sidewalk doormen arranged the people into lines on the sidewalk. These employees were supposed to be tall young men "of the clean-cut college type." For this job, the company wanted "optimistic and smiling, extremely courteous" men who were "at home in making contacts with those who are strangers to him." On inclement days, they would let people form lines inside the lobby before buying tickets.

As patrons stepped up to the small ticket lobby, the always-polite cashiers asked, "How many, please?" B&K told its managers: "Cashiers should be young ladies about twenty-five years of age, having a very pleasing personality and voice. It is not necessary that they be beautiful girls, but should be of a refined type, not using too much rouge or lipstick, and wearing their hair in a conservative style rather than in an extreme fashion." They weren't allowed to chew gum or wear flashy jewelry.

Tickets were never sold on a reserved basis—the same price would get you a seat anywhere in the theater. This policy was rooted in A.J. Balaban's philosophy that "every man was king." Balaban & Katz also didn't raise prices for any movies that might be considered special. "If a house has the confidence of its patrons, and raises prices for special pictures, the patrons immediately judge pictures by the prices asked," Barney Balaban said.

Moviegoers could get a bargain on ticket prices if they showed up early and caught a matinee. Although *We Moderns* was shown five times a day—always followed by a Felix the Cat cartoon—only three of these screenings were part of a show featuring the full array of entertainment. Audience members who showed up at 2 o'clock would see the movie as soon as they were guided to their seats by an usher.

The ushers were among the Uptown's most important employees, given how much contact they had with customers. For this job, Balaban & Katz urged managers to hire young men, seventeen to twenty-one years old, about 5 foot 7, weighing 135 to 145 pounds, who were "keenly alert" and looked as if they came from "wholesome homes of refinement." The company put them through military-style training. "Boys were well drilled, smartly uniformed and coached continuously in their approach and service to the patrons," A.J. Balaban said. They were trained to use hand signals to communicate with fellow ushers. For example, an usher summoned a manager by putting his right hand's index finger on his sleeve. Ushers memorized the exact phrases they would say to patrons in various scenarios: "Seats are this way, please." "Kindly remain in the rear of the aisle, please, until the next usher can seat you." "I beg your pardon, sir." The ushers were also trained about what *not* to do: "Never smack thighs. Never snap your fingers. Never cough or clear throat. Do not create disturbance." And as usual, accepting tips was forbidden, along with any form of romance: "You are warned not to carry on conversation with patrons, particularly girls. Brief, courteous, businesslike answers should serve. Any flirtatious conduct on your part, or suggestion thereof, will cause immediate dismissal."

Ushers were ordered to maintain a "faultless" appearance. Before going on duty, they were supposed to ask themselves: "Are my hands and face clean; are my shoes clean and shined; is my linen clean; is my uniform adjusted properly; is my hair cut properly?" And, like other employees, ushers were urged to develop a resplendent personality. As the company explained: "We must at all times remember that our patrons visit us during their playtime. A radiant personality dominating our organization will add to their pleasure while the

A full-page 1926 ad hypes the Uptown's first year and the future of Balaban & Katz.

lack of this element may disturb them to the extent that they cannot fully enjoy the entertainment which we have provided for them."

While a show was in progress, ushers watched for disturbances, like people shelling peanuts or rustling paper bags or parcels. "I am sorry, sir (or ma'am). You are annoying those around you," they would say. Instead of shushing noisy patrons, the ushers would say, "Pardon me, sir. Please be quiet during the performance. Thank you."

In all situations, Balaban & Katz counseled its workers to be lenient, explaining: "Tolerance is an indication of broadmindedness and human understanding. It is the ability to maintain your self-control and poise in the face of exceedingly trying circumstances." Even as Balaban & Katz prepared its employees for difficult situations, it also emphasized how the experience of seeing a show in its glorious movie palaces brought people together: "We must be ever mindful of the cardinal fact that our patrons are seeking pleasant entertainment and diversion," the company stated. "For the time being, they have put aside their own home or business cares to live for a few hours in a world of music, fiction, and beauty."

In February 1926, audience members who watched the entire variety show from beginning to end were treated to two hours and twenty minutes of entertainment. The guiding force behind these shows was Frank Cambria, who oversaw Balaban & Katz's stage shows for years, drawing on his experiences as an architect, portrait painter, and theatrical scenic artist. *Moving Picture World* called him "a recognized leader in the science of charting what the motion picture patrons want in a theater and an entertainment." Cambria believed that each show should have one unified theme, a motif connecting the settings, music, and costumes, but he said the live show should not refer to the plot in the feature movie. "I feel quite strongly that there is place for but one plot in a performance, and when that performance takes place in a film house, that one must be the plot of the motion picture," he said.

The show began with the platform rising from the orchestra pit. The conductor controlled the movement of his platform as well as the orchestra's platform with push buttons. B&K warned its managers to look out for conductors who went a little wild with this equipment. "Your attention is particularly called to the very destructive habit of some conductors in using the stop push buttons and reversing the mechanism too rapidly which causes great strain on the mechanism and might result in burning out some of your electrical coils," the company said. Whenever a movie was showing on the screen, managers were told to make sure the musicians and their music stands were low enough that they didn't block the audience members' sightlines.

As the orchestra played, the Uptown's lighting system displayed colors around the auditorium to reflect the mood of the music, using the world's largest and most sophisticated stage lighting board at the time. "The perfect harmony of the music and the lighting holds the huge audiences spellbound," noted a 1926 article in *Chicago Engineering Works Review*.

During some of the Uptown's shows, the music and entertainment was broadcast live to radio listeners. WEBH, a radio station based at the Edgewater Beach Hotel, had a small studio above the Lawrence Avenue Lobby. With a microphone on the stage, WEBH picked up the sounds of the performances. The *Tribune's* radio columnist, Elmer Douglass, was impressed by the classical music he heard during one broadcast. "We of the radio audience could not see the mystic blue-purple lights within the theater's dome, nor watch the moving scene, but instead we were right there in the orchestra pit with our ears flirting with the instruments," he wrote. These broadcasts ceased in 1928 when WEBH shut down.

The orchestra's overture was followed by a five-minute "weekly." By 1926, these newsreels were actually being distributed twice a week, presenting "picture-stories of the current events and topics of the day." Newsreels featured "exceptionally rapid changes," so B&K urged theaters to prepare musical accompaniment with a stopwatch, carefully making

Uptown's original Wurlitzer organ console, with four manuals, survives in San Jose's California Theatre.

sure that the music changed to match the news stories on the screen.

And then the star organist Jesse Crawford played the Uptown's Wurlitzer organ for six minutes. According to the schedule, Crawford would play "Sleepy Time Gal." But a *Variety* critic who attended the show reported that Crawford actually did a comical performance of "Ain't It a Grand and Glorious Feeling." It was this critic's favorite part of the whole show. "To the accompaniment of screen drawings and captions, Crawford interprets the average man's feelings when his wife drags him to the concert, the lecture and the opera," he wrote. "Then into a pop number that doesn't strain the intellect."

Billed as "The Poet of the Organ," Crawford was one of Chicago's most famous people at the time. Balaban & Katz had hired him away from Los Angeles theater owner Sid Grauman, of Grauman's Chinese and Egyptian theaters fame, in 1921 to play at the Tivoli and Chicago theaters. In 1923, Crawford married fellow organist Helen Anderson, and they became one of show business's best-paid "Mr. and Mrs." teams. At the Uptown, Crawford played the Mighty Wurlitzer. "Part one-man band, part symphony orchestra, part sound-

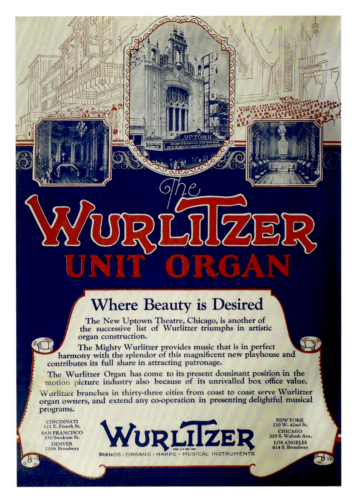

Many suppliers proudly advertised their contributions to the Uptown to entice more clients.

effects department, the Wurlitzer was one of the most versatile instruments ever devised by man," Ben Hall wrote in *The Best Remaining Seats.* With its thousands of pipes, the organ could make the sounds of everything from glockenspiels and gongs to galloping horses and auto horns ("honk-honk" as well as "ah-oo-gah"). "There was virtually no mood or situation on the silent screen that a quick-thinking and agile organist couldn't heighten with some musical theme and mechanical effect from the Wurlitzer Hope-Jones Unit Orchestra's bag of tricks," Hall wrote.

During the February 1926 show, Crawford was followed by a troupe of 20 actors—including "the Six Dancing Scovell Girls"—performing *The Honeymoon,* a "tuneful merry miniature musical comedy" by Will M. Hough, with four acts running 35 minutes. (The Chicago-born Hough had co-written the lyrics for the 1909 hit "I Wonder Who's Kissing Her Now.") A *Variety* critic said *The Honeymoon* "meant little or nothing, although done on the gorgeous scale of scenic effects in which the B&K production department is so proficient."

Then came the feature movie. *We Moderns* starred Colleen Moore, who had begun her career as an extra at the nearby Essanay studio. A self-proclaimed flapper with bobbed hair, she'd was now one of the era's most popular actresses. Explaining the attitude of flappers, Moore said, "What everyday, healthy normal little girl doesn't sort of like to be smart and naughty?" In *We Moderns,* Moore played "a young woman who spurns her childhood sweetheart to attach herself to a large group of riotous, semi-artistic young people and becomes infatuated with a superficial poet and critic." And she eventually survives a dirigible crash. "She's Swift! She's Smart! She's Daring!—But, Oh-h! How Lovable She Is!" the Uptown's ad proclaimed. No known copies exist today of this

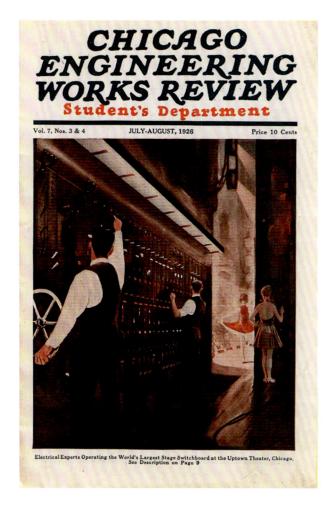

Advances at the Uptown in stage and auditorium lighting as well as air cooling were news in trade journals.

seven-reel feature.

At three of the day's screenings, *We Moderns* had a time slot of 73 minutes. The projectionist up in the kinobooth was apparently running the film at the standard speed of 90 feet per minute, which translates into 24 frames per second. But curiously, the schedule indicates that the film was sometimes shown at slightly slower speeds, stretching out its duration (and making Colleen Moore's movements a bit less lively).

Showing movies at a fast speed was a common practice, but B&K ordered its employees not to do it. "Over-speeding projection produces a ridiculous, jumpy, rapid and mechanical-like motion of the characters, rather laughable at times," the company explained. "It is extremely annoying to a patron seriously interested in the picture and many titles cannot be read, thereby breaking the continuity of the story." The company also warned against showing a film at too slow of a speed, because the opening and closing of the projector's lens could create flashes of light and dark. "Flicker is very serious in that it produces an eye strain, which in the early days of motion pictures kept many away from theaters," the company said. Despite these edicts, the Uptown's conductor stand on the orchestra lift had dials allowing the conductor to change a film's projection speed as well.

B&K managers were told to watch out for other problems with films. Was the image out of focus? That could be the result of a bad lens or the wrong combination of lens. If a picture did not look bright enough, the company suggested changing the type of lamp, the carbons, or the condenser combination, or increasing the amperage. Rewinding a film improperly could scratch its emulsion. Problems with a projector's teeth could damage a film's sprocket holes. "This causes a jumpy picture and is responsible for many breaks," the company said. "The effect of watching

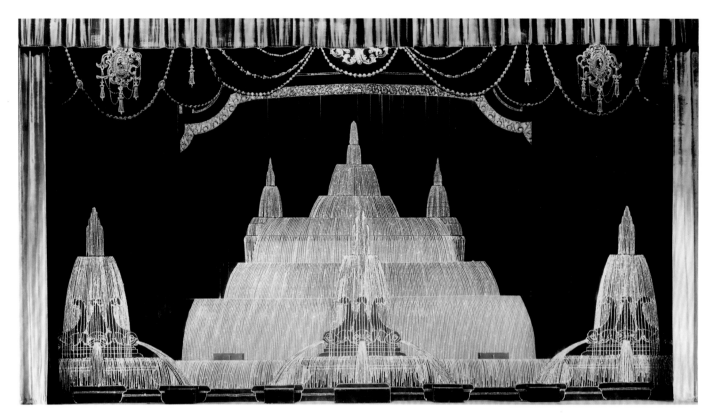

A hardboard cutout scene with a "fountain" made of crystal beads, dropped in front of black velvet curtain.

a jumpy picture is the same as trying to read a book or newspaper on a rough riding train." To ensure the quality of their work, projectionists at bigger theaters like the Uptown were equipped with field glasses to help them see the screen from their lofty perch, 160 feet from the screen.

During the movie, the orchestra and organist played a live soundtrack while the silent images flashed on the screen. Balaban & Katz said the music should harmonize with the emotions in each scene of a movie. The music should be well timed, without any abrupt changes. A theme should be heard throughout the movie, along with specific motifs for characters. And while the music should add to a movie's atmosphere, audience members shouldn't be "consciously aware of the musical accompaniment." Ideally, the music—whether it was played by an orchestra or an organist—should include classical music as well as "lighter popular numbers." Organists were discouraged from improvising "in such a way as to distract and confuse the audience." According to theater historian Joe DuciBella, organists would play a portion of the musical accompaniment for movies—especially when the orchestra musicians were given a fifteen-minute break following forty-five minutes of work.

When the performance ended for the night, the fire curtain was lowered, raised, and then lowered again. During bad weather, the marquee lights stayed illuminated until all patrons had left. The footman stayed until the last patrons left the theater. It was important for the Uptown to end its show by midnight so as to avoid paying overtime to employees represented by unions. At the end of the day, the cleaning staff often found chewing gum wrappers and candy boxes—evidence that people really did snack during shows, despite the lack of concession stands.

During the first week of February 1926, *Variety's* dyspeptic critic was unenthusiastic about the show, a feeling that was apparently shared by at least some audience members. "This reviewer overheard two different comments from the ladies, which, boiled down, were to the effect that the program was 'punk,'" the critic wrote.

That same week, Balaban & Katz announced it was becoming a "national organization," with Frank Cambria moving to New York to oversee

This backdrop could be lit from behind. It framed the full setup for any band onstage.

live shows for theaters across the country. "This move was inevitable," an ad said. "It was just as illogical to create costly productions for our three large Chicago theatres and then abandon them as it would be to produce a great motion picture for a few theatres and then discard it. It was really a waste of artistic and creative effort." The company assured Chicagoans that "Chicago is directly responsible for this theatrical development." But author Ben Hall concluded: "Chicago was the loser in the deal." In Hall's 1961 history of movie palaces, he pointed out just how much talent Chicago lost in 1926. Along with Cambria, Sam Katz was heading to New York, and the star organist Jesse Crawford would soon follow.

Balaban & Katz became even more entwined with Paramount in a deal that year. Paramount bought a controlling interest in B&K, while Barney Balaban became a $10 million shareholder in Paramount, owning more of the company than anyone except its top mogul, Adolph Zukor. Balaban stayed in Chicago to continue overseeing the B&K theaters, but Katz moved to New York, taking nearly his entire staff to run the national Publix theater chain. As the *Collyer's Eye* newspaper observed, "The Chicago crowd barged into Paramount with their big, ornate theater ideas."

According to author Hall, "Sam Katz considered himself the victor in the Paramount-Balaban & Katz-Publix machinations." Reflecting on his rise to this powerful position, Katz said: "One is shoved into a job bigger than he is used to. Then he has pride in doing it, so he drives himself along and hard. The effort makes him more capable and bigger things come his way." Over the next five years, Katz would double the Publix empire's size, to 1,000 movie houses. He controlled nearly every detail of the entertainment at theaters throughout the chain, establishing himself as one of the movie world's most powerful business titans and creative forces. According to historian Douglas Gomery, the merger between Balaban & Katz and Famous Players-Lasky created the world's most powerful movie company.

Not everyone liked those big, ornate theaters—or their style of entertainment. In a scathing 1927 essay for the *American Mercury*, W.A.S. Douglas lamented that Chicago's movie palaces were stealing audiences away from vaudeville houses. Douglas, a former editor for

Pathé Weekly who had directed movies and was now the *Baltimore Sun's* Chicago correspondent, directed his ire at the mogul of B&K's parent corporation. "Adolph Zukor, the presiding genius of Paramount, has erected and is engaged in erecting such mammoth sinks of movie imbecility all over this land and Europe," Douglas wrote. "In them his super pictures glide over the sprockets to the music of super orchestras. His audiences loll in armchairs while mellow lighting effectively rests their eyes. George F. Babbitt and his family are lulled into something akin to a hop dream without the pernicious after-effects. … The kaleidoscope glides in perfectly blended colors before them. They see nothing that makes the slightest strain on their minds." Douglas was alluding to Sinclair Lewis's 1922 novel *Babbitt,* whose title character had become emblematic of professional men who conformed unthinkingly to vacuous middle-class standards.

In spite of Douglas's cynical attitude, countless Chicagoans treasured the experience of stepping inside a Balaban & Katz movie palace. One of them, Jo Lewinski, recalled: "Every day of my life for 17 years I could look down the street from my gray wooden porch and see the Uptown Theatre in Chicago. I used to think that the sun rose and set over its huge, rounded roof. The Uptown was part of the landscape of my childhood. Its glorious decor and double feature movies fueled my imagination, decorated my dreams, enriched my life. There was nothing so magical as the lights of the marquee beckoning and enticing in the night—hundreds of mesmerizing little globes strobing seductively, come hither."

After the initial hoopla about the Uptown's grand opening died down, Balaban & Katz struggled to fill the Uptown's 4,000 seats. In March 1926, *Variety* reported that the Uptown was "flopping badly." The trade magazine stated: "It can't be said that this house is doing so well. Right now there are 15,000 seats competing in the neighborhood, with more springing up almost daily." To succeed, the Uptown needed to pull in people from other parts of Chicago, as it had during its grand opening. But with so much competition, that was no easy task.

Attendance improved when the Uptown hosted early afternoon teas. "The matinees have become something of a minor social event with the housewives in the Uptown neighborhood," *Variety* reported. "Balaban and Katz conceived pink teas with the mezzanine foyer converted into a drawing room for the afternoon. The hand-out has made a powerful appeal. This pink tea racket makes a good flash and probably doesn't cost as much as, for instance, the souvenirs given away in ballrooms. It looks like a great investment. Strictly a feminine draw with female attendants to pour the beverage."

And then in late March 1926, Balaban & Katz made a change that would pull in bigger crowds: The Uptown hired bandleader Bennie Krueger, who as a member of the Original Dixieland Jazz Band in 1920 was one of the first saxophonists to play on a jazz record. "Orchestrations are practically perfect, with all the pep in the world," *Variety's* critic wrote after seeing him at the Uptown. "Bennie swings in on one chorus in each song to display his majestic power over the reed but shows his sporting blood by saving his applause bows to be taken with the entire orchestra." The critic predicted that Krueger "will have a pretty good following in a short time." And that's just what the Uptown needed, *Variety* wrote: "The theater needs a steady drawing attraction, and Bennie Krueger may furnish it as soon as the neighborhood gets chummy with him. Nothing can be said against his music."

For a while that spring, Krueger's group included Benny Goodman, a sixteen-year-old clarinetist who would gain renown as the "King of Swing." Goodman remembered his Uptown Theatre gig in a memoir (co-written with Irving Kolodin): "Krueger was the M.C. and also played sax solos now and then, as did Victor Young, the composer of 'Sweet Sue,' who was the first fiddle player in the band. The idea was that they had one hot man and one straight man in each section, and they took me on to have a crack at the hot work in the reeds. … In addition to playing jazz we played the usual overtures and operatic arrangements, but it wasn't the kind of playing I cared much about since I always liked to get off more than you could in that kind of a band."

Goodman moved on to other gigs, but Krueger was just getting started at the Uptown. By July 1926, he was drawing large audiences to the theater. "The Uptown, Balaban & Katz's most beautiful theater, is doing capacity these more or less sultry days," *Variety* reported. "Answer lies in the unprecedented popularity of Bennie Krueger and his now augmented orchestra more than in anything else. ... Krueger and his 22-piece orchestra on the stage are growing daily more popular. ... Krueger himself is one of the finest saxophone artists in this country, and that is not sheer enthusiasm. His personality and appearance are also a factor in his success."

Krueger was Uptown's regular bandleader through 1928. But the theater occasionally booked others—including the "King of Jazz" Paul Whiteman (who commissioned and premiered George Gershwin's *Rhapsody in Blue*). A.J. Balaban recalled paying as much as $10,000 a week to get Whiteman to perform in B&K's theaters. When Whiteman was the star attraction at the Uptown in late 1926, ads didn't bother to mention the singers in his band—Bing Crosby and Al Rinker. The twenty-three-year-old Crosby wasn't famous yet. He and Rinker had played with Whiteman for the first time just a week earlier, at the Tivoli, a few months after making their first record.

Crosby made another appearance at the Uptown a few years later with actress Dixie Lee, whom he married in 1930. "My parents were dating and attending one of the old vaudeville shows at the Uptown," Constance A. Coultry recalled. "In those days the stars would come out to the lobby and greet the audience members after the shows. They had attended a performance starring a big star named Dixie Lee ... and were wondering who that nice young man accompanying her was." The Uptown's longtime stage manager, Frank Carsen, remembered Crosby visiting the theater, as well as John Barrymore and the legendary Hollywood

Popular band leader Bennie Krueger feted in 1926.

couple Mary Pickford and Douglas Fairbanks. While some of the celebrities simply visited the Uptown to take in a show—rolling up to the entrance in their chauffeured limousines—others took the stage.

The Four Marx Brothers—Groucho, Chico, Harpo, and Zeppo—advertised as the "world's funniest fellows," delivered their live comedy show at the Uptown in April 1928. They performed *Spanish Nights,* a show that they recently premiered at the Coronado Theatre in Rockford. Like many entertainers presented by Balaban & Katz, the Marxes took their tour across the city, playing a week at downtown's Chicago Theatre and a week on the South Side at the Tivoli.

Along with some new bits, *Spanish Nights* included scenes from *The Cocoanuts,* the brothers' Broadway show from 1925 and 1926. *The Cocoanuts* would become the Marx Brothers' feature film debut with a 1929 screen version. The new two-act musical revue, running forty minutes, had a cast of twenty-five, including the matronly

A 1929 ad hypes the Marx Brothers' first film release.

Margaret Dumont, who later starred in seven Marx Brothers movies, usually playing stuffy rich widows who were wooed and insulted by Groucho.

The Marx Brothers appeared one at a time in the opening scene, as each of them sought work from a producer seated at a desk. "All conversation is worked in rhyme," *Variety* reported. "The finish of this scene is handled by Harpo doing his pantomime of drinking ink, wiping his lips with a blotter, sticking pens in the desk and spitting in a desk drawer." Reviewing a performance at the Chicago Theatre, *Variety* reported that Groucho "was a riot every time he mentioned the crime situation" in Chicago.

Other notable entertainers who performed at the Uptown during its first years included Jackie Coogan, the boy who starred as the title character of Charlie Chaplin's 1921 movie *The Kid*. He appeared for five days in 1928. And Ruth Etting, billed as "Chicago's singing sweetheart," played the Uptown in 1928, performing in a "novel, brilliant stage revue."

By that time, major changes were afoot in the world of movies. In November 1927, the Garrick Theatre in the Loop began showing *The Jazz Singer* starring Al Jolson, a film that dramatically changed what audiences expected when they went to the movies. The Warner Bros. production featured the sound of Jolson singing and speaking words that would soon be famous: "Wait a minute, wait a minute. You ain't heard nothing yet!" These sounds were recorded on discs, which were synchronized with select scenes. "Al Jolson, large as life and twice as natural!" *Tribune* critic Mae Tinée wrote. "So good is he that it's hard to believe he isn't before you in person. ... Then, the Vitaphone steps in and, presto, permits you to HEAR him sing his beloved songs for you. AND it's Al Jolson singing—not just a record. The illusion is perfect." It was an instant hit, drawing big crowds to the Garrick.

For a while, the Uptown couldn't compete with this new technology. By April 1928, *The Jazz Singer* was showing at other neighborhood theaters around the city: the Granada, Sheridan, Marbro, and Avalon. Meanwhile, the Uptown featured live performances by George Jessel, who had originated the title role in the original stage production of *The Jazz Singer* before turning down a chance to star in the movie.

That summer, the Uptown hyped its live music, bringing back bandleader Paul Whiteman. It later announced an enlarged orchestra led by Italian conductor Ulderico Marcelli. "Another great step in the Uptown Theatre's march of supremacy," an ad proclaimed. A report in *Variety* revealed why the Uptown suddenly had more musicians in the pit: Balaban & Katz had dismissed its orchestra at McVicker's Theatre, a movie house the company partially owned in the Loop, when it showed *Street Angel* with a synchronized musical score and sound effects. Those musicians were no longer needed, but some found work at the Uptown thanks to the intervention of James C. Petrillo, leader of the Chicago Federation of Musicians.

In August 1928, B&K wired the Uptown and other theaters for sound, adding speaker systems. And on September 1, 1928, the Uptown showed its first sound movie. With typical hyperbole, the theater's ad proclaimed: "Come Early Today for the Greatest Thrill in the History of Motion Picture Entertainment!" Actually, *Warming Up* didn't have any audible dialogue, but Paramount's baseball movie did have a synchronized musical score with sound effects. "Our perfected equipment—the latest and newest Sound Devices—transforms the screen into living, breathing persons," B&K declared. "It will seem as if real humans stood before you." A day after *Warming Up* opened, another ad reported that audiences were "cheering madly," just like the baseball fans on the movie screen. The Uptown also showed Fox Movietone newsreels. For many local audience members, it was undoubtedly the first time they'd ever seen *and heard* news events and famous people. But even as the Uptown entered the age of sound, it was still presenting live entertainment, including Bennie Krueger and a curious hybrid of recorded and live music. Marcelli conducted the Uptown Theatre Symphony Orchestra as it played along a Movietone recording of Richard Bonelli, a star singer with the Chicago Civic Opera.

In the same week when sound movies debuted at the Uptown, musicians went on strike against roughly 250 smaller neighborhood theaters across the city, demanding guarantees that these theaters would continue employing at least six musicians. The strike ended a week later when these theaters agreed to employ at least four musicians for the next year. Petrillo sounded confident that musicians would continue working in theaters, in spite of the new audio systems. "We don't fear them—they are canned music," he said. Petrillo said these machines made "coarse, grinding noises" inferior to live music. "They are new, a novelty that is both wonderful and awe-inspiring," he said. "But the sharp edge of their newfound popularity will wear off in due time. When that day comes the living, breathing player of the fiddle and horn will once more enter into his inheritance."

Later in September, the Uptown showed a movie with audible dialogue in some scenes, *State Street Sadie* starring Myrna Loy. "Hear their voices in the thrilling scenes of this night-life adventure," an ad said. "Our perfected Vitaphone makes it real as life."

In New York, Sam Katz was ordering sound movies of performances by musicians and vaudeville entertainers. These short films could be shown in place of actual performers—a big savings.

By 1929, most Publix theaters across the country had discarded live entertainment, but it continued at the Uptown. Tom Mix, who starred in hundreds of westerns, performed with his "wonder horse" Tony at the Uptown in 1929. "See Him Ride! Rope! Shoot!" an ad proclaimed. Mix, touted as the "world's greatest cowboy star," lodged at the Lawrence Hotel, 1020 West Lawrence Avenue. It's unknown where Tony stayed.

For a while in 1929, the Uptown hosted "Whoopee" time at the weirdly specific time of 9:39 p.m. on weeknights. Advertised as "an hour of rollicking entertainment," it was designed to boost late-evening attendance. "Avoid the early evening throngs—come a little later, enjoy a dozen added novelty surprises added to the regular program," an ad suggested. The nightly "whoopee" consisted of "10 minutes of happy singing, 5 minutes of rollicking comedy, 15 minutes of red-hot syncopation, a dash of beauty, a pinch of wit."

Nationally, movie attendance hit one of its all-time highs in 1930, when theaters sold 90 million tickets a week. That September, as the Uptown Theatre celebrated its fifth anniversary with a giant birthday cake and an array of movies and live entertainment, the *Uptown News* observed that the movie palace had been a major factor in the neighborhood's development. "Community leaders find the theater an asset to the shopping district and giving impetus to trade and attracting people from other parts of Chicago and acquainting them with Uptown," the newspaper said. By that time, the Uptown had sold nearly 18 million tickets.

The Uptown ended 1930 with a week of performances by the popular Chicago-born Harry Blackstone Sr., who was billed as the "World's Most Baffling Magician." The Uptown's ad promised: "He will astound you! His feats are strange! Mysterious! Unaccountable!" As Blackstone later embarked on a national tour of Publix Theatres, a promotional card announced that his week at the Uptown had broken a house record with a total attendance of 121,833 and box office receipts of $42,000. It seemed like the Uptown was a place where magic happened.

CHAPTER FIVE
CHANGING TIMES

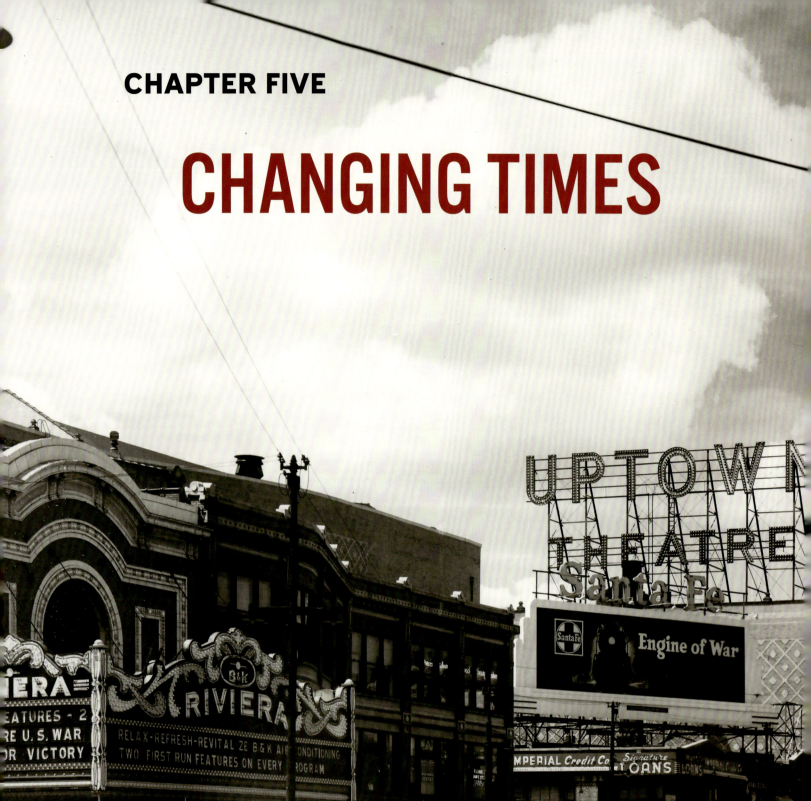

Summer day in 1943 on Broadway, looking north to Lawrence Avenue and the Uptown Theatre.

'We took all this for granted.'

As the country fell into the Great Depression, the Uptown continued making whoopee—for the time being, anyway. One of the era's most popular bandleaders, Paul Ash, brought his "Merry Mad Stage Show" to the Uptown for a week starting in 1931—the first time he had ever headlined at a Chicago theater outside of the Loop. Born in Germany and raised in Milwaukee, Ash was nicknamed "The Rajah of Jazz." He was known for his long, red hair—long by that era's standards—and his exuberant style of conducting. "The first notes of his orchestra electrify him," the *Balaban & Katz Magazine* said. "He becomes taut; nervous energy flashes from him, like live sparks. Swaying, stamping, smiling, coaxing, cajoling every movement of his brawny body carries a demand or an appeal to his 'merry musicians.'" Rose Wandel was about ten when she saw Paul Ash's show at the Uptown. "The chorus of dancing girls presented a number in which they were dressed as snowballs, and then they threw cotton snowballs to the audience at the end of their number. … The theater itself was truly a palace. Balaban & Katz really gave their customers a period of illusion and feeling grand."

A week after Ash's exit, the "'Boop-a-Doop' Star" made her entrance. Helen Kane looked and sounded a lot like Betty Boop, who made her screen debut six months earlier in a Fleischer Studios cartoon. Kane claimed that the filmmakers had stolen her "boop-oop-a-doop," but she failed to convince a judge. At the Uptown, she performed with bandleader Al Kvale, a Minnesota congressman's son who abandoned his plans for a law career to play jazz. If any children wanted to see Betty Boop's real-life counterpart, they would have had trouble getting in—the show also included *Inspiration,* a movie starring Greta Garbo as a "kept woman" working as an artist's model in Paris. City censors ordered that all screenings would be "adults only."

One of the greatest musical moments in the Uptown's early history was surely the weeklong residency of Duke Ellington and His New York Cotton Club Orchestra, which performed at the theater in early 1931, advertised as "THE HOTTEST BAND IN THE WORLD!" Ellington had launched his tour of Chicago at the Loop's Oriental Theatre, causing a *Chicago Defender* critic to exclaim: "What rhythm! What harmony! What unison!" After a week at the Oriental and a week at the South Side's Regal Theatre, Ellington brought his players to the Uptown, playing "Strike Up the Band," "Ring Dem Bells," "Black and Tan Fantasy." The show featured vocalist Ivie Anderson, who a year later would sing on the recording of a new Ellington composition: "It Don't Mean a Thing (If It Ain't Got That Swing)." Ellington was not the only notable African American artist who performed early on the Uptown's stage. Singer-actress Ethel Waters brought her touring show *Rhapsody in Black* to the Uptown in August 1932 with a cast that included "Queen of the Trumpet" Valaida Snow and the Berry Brothers dancing trio. Later that year, James A. Mundy, director and minister of music at the South Side's Olivet Baptist Church, led his massed vocal choir at the Uptown.

By this time, the Publix–Balaban & Katz chain dominated moviegoing in Chicago. At the end of 1931, the company had thirty-six theaters advertising in local newspapers. (And that doesn't include the Regal, which B&K planned to close—only to reverse the decision when the surrounding Black community protested.) The company's newest theater was the Southtown, which opened Christmas Day in the South Side's Englewood neighborhood. Not surprisingly, B&K's ads called it "the most glorious sight America has ever seen." It featured an amenity that B&K hadn't bothered to include with the Uptown: "Free Parking on Premises for 1,000 Cars." The 3,206-seat Southtown couldn't hold as many people as the Uptown, but its floors covered more square feet. By that measure, it was the biggest theater Balaban & Katz would ever build.

The Southtown was the sixth Chicago movie palace Balaban & Katz constructed since opening the Uptown more than six years earlier. These castles stood at various strategic locations across the city, each reigning over a different fiefdom of

CHICAGO AERIAL SURVEY COMPANY PHOTO

By the early 1930s, the area surrounding the Uptown Theatrre (lower left) was densely built.

moviegoers. The Rapp & Rapp firm designed the Southown as well as the Oriental, the Gateway, and the Norshore. Other notable architects drew up the plans for B&K's other palaces. J.E.O. Pridmore designed the Nortown. And John Eberson designed the Paradise, regarded by some as B&K's most lavish.

Balaban & Katz also bought theaters from other companies, including thirteen constructed by Lubliner & Trinz. By December 1931, B&K's Chicago-area theaters (including three in the suburbs) had more than 89,000 seats. The Uptown was the biggest—the region's only movie house with more than 4,000 seats. When it opened in 1925, the 4,320-seat Uptown was the world's second-largest movie theater in terms of seating capacity. Only the 5,230-seat Capitol Theatre in New York was bigger. But since then, two New York theaters had surpassed the Uptown: the 5,105-seat Hippodrome Theatre (which had opened in 1905 but didn't show movies until 1926) and the 5,920-seat Roxy Theatre. The biggest theater of all, the 5,960-seat Radio City Music Hall, would open at the end of 1932.

But America's theater building boom was crashing because of the Great Depression. The Southtown would be the last movie palace ever built in Chicago. Nationwide, the number of movie theaters peaked at 23,344 in 1928, but the total was nearly cut in half by 1932. As the industry fell on hard times, a writer for the *Kansas City Star* looked back on the extravagant projects pushed by Sam Katz and other moguls: "Nothing was too expensive, nothing was too gaudy. They made a gasping public wonder where the money was all coming from. It might have been better if the magnates had paused to ask themselves that question. It became practically impossible to remain a prosperous independent theater operator. The biography of such a man would have begun by saying: 'I am a fugitive from a chain theater gang.'"

Smaller theaters had a tough time competing with Hollywood's Big Five: Paramount, Warner Bros., 20th Century Fox, RKO, and Loew's, owner of MGM. These movie-making companies also owned theaters—including nearly all of the first-run movie palaces—and they set the terms for showing their movies. "When times were bad ... the Big Five squeezed every possible dime from their films in their theaters before permitting an independent theater to book at all," historian Douglas Gomery wrote.

During those tense times in the theater business, the Uptown faced a smelly nuisance, when a stench bomb went off during a show in October 1932. Moviegoers momentarily fled, but the show went on when the ventilation system was cranked up and the foul odor quickly dissipated. Stink bombs, as they were also known, hit the Marbro and Tivoli, too. Who was responsible? *Variety* suggested that these B&K movie palaces were being attacked by independent exhibitors, who were angry about a schedule dictating that the smallest theaters wouldn't get a chance to show movies until fourteen weeks after they opened in the biggest theaters.

But this may have actually been the latest salvo in a long-running feud between theater owners and unions. Don Helgeson, a union projectionist who later worked at the Uptown, said the theater was hit by the stink bombs more than once. Helgeson (speaking in 2025 at the age of ninety) said the attacks were a union tactic to pressure the theater's owners against hiring nonunion projectionists. The owners often complained about union rules—

Musician Al Kvale outside the theater in a publicity shot.

especially the requirement that two union members work in every projection booth, even if it took only one person to run a projector. Theater owners tried to scrap rules like this in 1927, locking out union members and shutting down Chicago's movie shows for six days. But the union wouldn't budge. In that era, Chicago's unions for projectionists and stagehands were reportedly led by thugs and controlled by the mob. Tommy Maloy, boss of Motion Picture Operators' Union Local 110, allegedly extorted Balaban & Katz, promising tranquility as long as he got paid off with regular kickbacks. Projectionists who challenged Tommy Maloy's union leadership ended up dead, and Maloy—who was suspected but never convicted in nine murders—was eventually gunned down himself in 1935.

The rule requiring two projectionists to work every movie would remain until 1975, but that didn't mean there were actually two people in every projection booth. Half of the paychecks were going to "no-show mob guys—real soldiers in the mob," according to a union member who went to prison for arson. "Yeah, that's true," Helgeson said. "They had this rule because the union was strong, and they were able to get two people on the job. They could put one movie operator in, and then a dunce who happened to be related to somebody. In some cases, that's the way it went. It was a phantom job."

Actor Francis X. Bushman (right) amid an Uptown display of Essanay and filmmaking history in 1938.

As listening to radio programs at home began to subtract audience numbers and as Paramount sank deeper into debt in the early 1930s, Sam Katz became the studio's production chief. He said audiences weren't in the mood for any more high-society movies. "With people out of work and those who still have jobs receiving salary cuts and wondering how much longer they are going to hold those jobs, I don't believe they want to go into a theater and see money scattered around like it was so much wastepaper," he said. Katz, facing criticism for the money he'd scattered around himself, resigned from Paramount in October 1932.

The same month, *Variety* reported that Paramount's Balaban & Katz subsidiary was losing $40,000 a week. Paramount Chairman Adolph Zukor remembered 1932 as the year when "the bottom dropped out." Two years into the Great Depression, a fourth of American workers were unemployed. Panicked people lined up outside banks to withdraw money—if they could. Spending cash on a night out at the movies was now an unaffordable luxury for many. In Chicago, the Uptown and its sister cinemas pitched their shows as a necessary form of escapism. "Millions Find Happiness in Balaban & Katz Theaters," one ad declared. "You, too, need the romance, the excitement, the relaxation that Balaban & Katz Theatres provide, as surely as you need food and lodging … and the prices are within the reach of everyone. Live two glorious hours or more in these great theaters. It will do your heart good."

The company decided a "big push" was needed to get moviegoers back into the Uptown. "Crowd luring stunts" were planned for the neighborhood—window shopping prizes, an "automobile parade with girls," and "extra illuminations everywhere." But Americans simply weren't going out as often as they used to. Sixty million movie tickets were sold each week in 1932—a 33 percent drop since 1928.

In November, B&K cut admission prices by about 10 percent; the Uptown charged sixty-five cents for shows after 2:30 p.m. The prices dropped again in December, falling to fifty cents. As the year ended, the Uptown presented a giant Christmas show with the stage "aglow with Christmas ornaments and trees of various hues and with brilliant lighting effects." But after some whoopee on New Year's Eve, live entertainment ceased at the Uptown—for the time being. The theater's ads promised a "BIG PROGRAM of Complete Motion Picture Entertainment." Along with the feature—Essanay Studios alum Wallace Beery in *Flesh*—the Uptown's "special added events" were all short films: Bing Crosby singing "Blue Is the Night," the Walt Disney cartoon *Flowers and Trees,* and the travelogue *Moscow, Heart of Soviet Russia.* "If the coming of sound caused the end of the stage show, the Great Depression buried it," Douglas Gomery wrote. "Orchestra pits were covered up; paint in the dressing rooms began to peel; and backstage became another storage room." Over the coming years, the Uptown occasionally brought back live shows—for example, the Three Stooges (Moe Howard, Larry Fine, and Curly Howard) performed there in 1936—but these revivals didn't last long.

After losing $21 million in 1932, Paramount-Publix went into receivership. Balaban & Katz was forced to cut costs at the Uptown and other theaters, eliminating jobs. Looking for other ways to make money, America's theaters started selling candy. And so, for the first time, the Uptown had concession stands. In the late 1930s, many theaters across the country sold another snack: popcorn. Soft drinks would be added after World War II, when sugar rationing ended.

Movie attendance began climbing again in 1934. It took years for the economy to recover, but even during tough times, many people *did* find movies to be an essential part of their lives. Hollywood was in a golden age, producing popular films that have endured as classics. As live entertainment vanished from all but a few movie theaters, smaller exhibitors offered two movies for the price of one. Balaban & Katz resisted for a while, but by 1936 the Uptown was offering double features. Two years later, the Illinois Congress of Parents and Teachers urged Chicago to outlaw double features, arguing they were a health hazard to children. Alderman John J. Grealis agreed, remarking: "They are tiresome, unhealthy, and a detriment to the community." But aldermen shelved the idea—reportedly under pressure from Paramount.

By this time, the Uptown may have become a bit less glamorous, but it still seemed magical to Eileen Levine, daughter of Benjamin Bloomfield, the Uptown's manager during the 1940s. "My memories were of a fairyland, a palace," she wrote years later. "He used to take me to work whenever there was a movie playing my mother felt was 'suitable.' ... My dad wore a tux to work, and I think even spats. He had one of the ushers watch me whenever I was there and of course I once got lost—I decided to 'help' the ushers check out the entire theater between shows and tagged along with them. I also remember the doorman in full uniform, almost like a Beefeater's uniform with long coat, etc." The Uptown's candy storeroom held a special fascination. It was, as she recalled, "Heaven to any child. Candy wall-to-wall and floor-to-ceiling."

Renovations in the 1940s and '50s were made to give the Uptown a more modern look. Some walls were repainted, and new drapes were hung. The capacity was increased slightly—from 4,320 to 4,381—and new seats were installed on the auditorium's main floor and mezzanine. A

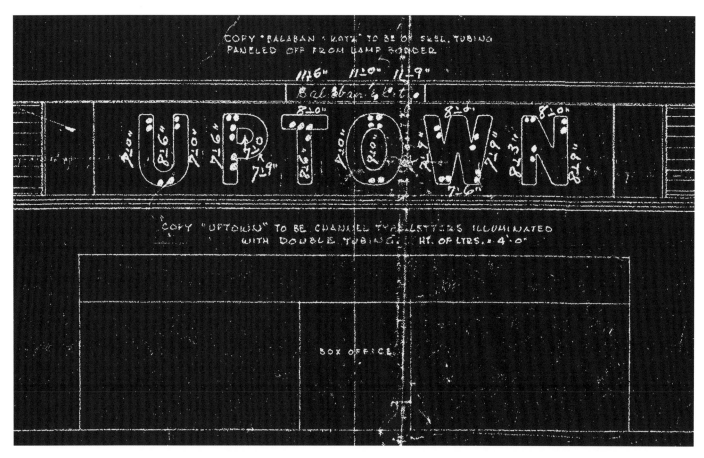

Detail of a 1948 White Way Sign Company drawing for a new marquee that was built for the Uptown.

new marquee was installed over the sidewalk on Broadway in 1948.

At the end of 1949, Balaban & Katz announced it was bringing back live entertainment to three of its biggest neighborhood movie houses, rotating shows at the Uptown, the Southtown, and the Marbro. A lineup packed with big stars—Mel Tormé, Ella Fitzgerald, and Henny Youngman—performed at the Uptown for a week starting on December 30, along with the Harmonicats, Hammond's Birds, Marty Gould and His Orchestra, and Chicago radio disc jockeys Linn Burton and Marty Hogan. And, of course, a movie, *The Lady Takes a Sailor,* was sandwiched in between the songs and jokes. But at the start of the new year, Balaban & Katz's experiment to reintroduce live shows came to an end. "They ran the circuit once, and they said, 'The hell with it. It's not working,'" historian Joe DuciBella said. "They could make as much money just running the movies as carrying and managing all of the staff."

Nationwide, movie ticket sales hit an all-time high in the years 1946 to 1948, but moviegoing was entering a new period of upheaval. One factor was the 1948 US Supreme Court decision involving Paramount, Uptown's corporate owner. The court said it was an illegal monopoly for studios to own theaters because Hollywood's big companies had too much power to decide where their movies were shown and how much tickets cost. "The practices were bald efforts to substitute monopoly for competition," Justice William O. Douglas wrote in the majority opinion. Paramount was forced to split into two companies: Paramount Pictures Corp. made movies, while United Paramount Theatres exhibited movies.

In the years that followed, studios made fewer movies. Ticket prices jumped. Weekly ticket sales plummeted from 90 million in 1948 to below 40 million in 1958. Television transformed from a novelty to a pervasive phenomenon. And millions of middle-class Americans moved out of city neighborhoods like Uptown, heading for the suburbs.

Uptown was no longer a magnet for shoppers.

During a housing shortage after World War II, the neighborhood's houses and hotels were divided to make room for more people. Many of these crowded apartments fell into disrepair. Poor white migrants from Appalachia moved in giving Uptown a reputation as "Jungles of Hillbillies," as the *Tribune* put it in a 1957 headline. The prejudice against these newcomers—mostly from Kentucky and West Virginia—was blatantly obvious in reporter Norma Lee Browning's sensational articles. She wrote about "clans of fightin', feudin' southern hillbillies and their shootin' cousins, who today constitute one of the most dangerous and lawless elements of Chicago's fast growing migrant population." But these Appalachians weren't to blame for the conditions of their buildings. Families spilled out of their crowded apartments onto the sidewalks and streets, and kids played amid trash and broken glass.

In the midst of these changes, the neighborhood remained a hub for entertainment. People still went dancing at the Aragon Ballroom. Over on Clark Street north of Lawrence Avenue, the old Rainbo Gardens reopened after World War II as a ballroom. In the 1950s, it hosted boxing and wrestling matches. And the Uptown and Riviera continued showing movies.

In the 1950s, the movie industry looked for ways to lure people back. One way of competing with television was to transform movie theaters into giant TV sets, showing special events you couldn't see at home. The Uptown installed closed-circuit television equipment in 1951. Paramount's system received a signal, recorded it on film, and projected it onto the screen within a minute.

The format's first success was a middleweight championship boxing match in New York between Sugar Ray Robinson and Randy Turpin in 1951. But Balaban & Katz officials were generally disappointed by the public's lukewarm response to closed-circuit events. Losing money, the company canceled plans to expand "theater television" to more locations. However, the Uptown continued showing special events from time to time. Ironically, as the Uptown competed with television, its corporate owner United Paramount Theatres merged in 1953 with the American Broadcasting Company.

Hollywood was also trying to make the moviegoing experience more spectacular. In March 1953, the Uptown showed *Bwana Devil,* the first feature using the three-dimensional Natural Vision process. Lions seemed to jump out of the screen when audience members used special glasses. Visiting Hollywood that spring, B&K executives John Balaban and David Wallerstein got a sneak peek at Warner Bros.' first 3D movie, *House of Wax,* which opened at the Uptown in May. Balaban said it was so vivid that he thought he smelled smoke when images of fire appeared on the screen. Balaban and Wallerstein predicted that 3D would change moviegoing even more than the advent of talkies in the late 1920s. During their California trip, they also saw a new format called CinemaScope. And in April 1953, 20th Century Fox executives used the Uptown to demonstrate these widescreen movies.

The screen used for the Uptown demonstration was 25 feet high—roughly the same height as the theater's old screen—but it stretched 65 feet across. Hundreds of invited guests watched panoramic scenes from two 20th Century Fox movies that wouldn't be released until later in the year: *The Robe,* a Biblical epic, and *How to Marry a Millionaire,* a romantic comedy starring Marilyn Monroe. A *Tribune* critic wrote that CinemaScope "seems well suited for films of a 'spectacle' nature." John Balaban said he believed CinemaScope would boost business at big old theaters. Wrote the *Daily News:* "The size of the CinemaScope screen makes the process impractical for small theaters. That is why it holds promise of bringing riches to the owners of the big movie palaces, which only a few months ago were being listed as white elephants by exhibitors."

CinemaScope condensed images as they were being filmed, squeezing a wide picture into a frame of standard 35-millimeter film. Then, when the movie was projected, special lenses stretched out images as they were thrown onto the screen.

CinemaScope was hyped as a competitor

to 3D movies, which were coming into vogue. The *Daily News* described the Uptown's CinemaScope demo as a "New 3-D Film." Its reporter commented: "There is a definite illusion of depth, but it was less forceful than that given by other forms of 3-D." In fact, there was nothing three-dimensional about these movies, other than the fact that the screen was a little curved. Audience members didn't need to wear special glasses.

While the Uptown continued to grind along in its dowdy and oversized way, other movie palaces were dying. It no longer made economic sense to build—or operate—theaters with thousands of seats. Ticket sales had plummeted since the peak of moviegoing right after World War II. In 1948, the average American purchased more than thirty-one tickets to the movies. By 1960, that number was only eleven. Meanwhile, the florid ornamentation of palaces like the Uptown had fallen out of favor, as theater designs got smaller, simpler, and sleeker, mirroring the main trends in architecture. Unlike Rapp & Rapp's gargantuan fantasies, which pieced together classic structures and finery from far-flung corners of the world and human history, modern buildings didn't refer to history at all. Everything was a clean slate. Chicago was becoming known for a new school of architecture, led by Ludwig Mies van der Rohe, who famously declared, "Less is more." Gewgaws gone. Steel, glass, and concrete in.

Movie palaces once regarded as masterpieces met the wrecking ball. On Chicago's West Side, architect John Eberson's Paradise, hailed as Balaban & Katz's most ornate theater when it opened in 1928, was demolished in 1956 by B&K to make way for a supermarket. A few years later, the company faced criticism as it prepared to tear down the Garrick Theatre in the Loop. Designed by Louis Sullivan as the Schiller Theatre, a German opera house, in 1891, it was converted into a movie theater by Balaban & Katz. It may not have met the typical definition of "movie palace," but it certainly was considered an architectural masterwork by some. The architectural photographer Richard Nickel and

HOWARD LYON/CHICAGO SUN-TIMES PHOTO

Protest against razing the Garrick Theatre in 1960.

other activists protested the demolition plans, picketing with signs that demanded to know: "Do We Dare Squander Chicago's Great Architectural Heritage?" The answer was yes. A lawyer for Balaban & Katz told city officials: "The fact that Mr. Sullivan designed this building is not legal or proper reason for denying to us the right to demolish it after it has outlived its usefulness and has become an economic burden." The outrage over the Garrick's destruction in 1960 and 1961 inspired a movement to Chicago's preserve historical buildings and add protections for landmark structures.

But the demolition of old movie houses continued. The fate of old theaters was not helped by a new trend: the multiplex. Giant one-screen theaters like the Uptown seemed more and more like relics. Another one of Balaban & Katz's classic movie palaces, the Tivoli, shut down in 1963. Three years later, it was razed to make way for a supermarket and parking lot.

Jim Small sat in the audience at the Uptown Theatre once a week—in spite of the fact that

JACK DYKINGA/CHICAGO SUN-TIMES PHOTO

Conditions in the Uptown neighborhood in the 1960s.

he watched movies all day long in his job as a projectionist for Balaban & Katz's downtown screening room. Small told a *Tribune* writer that he liked to see how the Uptown's crowd reacted to movies in comparison with the "cool, collected viewers" at the company's private screenings. He remembered, for example, watching the 1955 film *Marty,* which would win the Academy Award for Best Picture. "There's a line in there, where Marty (played by Ernest Borgnine) complains to his mother because when he gets home from a hard day's work he is fed a dinner out of a can," Small said. "Downtown, that didn't cause a ripple of reaction in the whole house. At the Uptown, the whole theater burst into applause."

Dave Syfczak, the Uptown's longtime caretaker, recalled seeing movies there growing up in the 1960s. "When I was a very small kid, I remember just running through this lobby to get to a seat," he said. "We took all this for granted. I didn't have an appreciation for it until I was a teenager and said, 'Man, this place is pretty cool.' The older I got, I knew that this place was kind of special. I didn't know it as a kid—I thought every neighborhood had one of these.

"This was a second-run house back then," he said. "If you wanted to see a first-run film, you had to go downtown. My mother dragged me here to *West Side Story.* She didn't want to go downtown to see it. But when it came to the neighborhood, then she wanted to come see it."

Audiences were far smaller than the Uptown's 4,000-plus capacity, so the stairs to the balcony were often roped off. But that didn't stop Jo Lewinski's father. He would unclasp the velvet rope, whisk his family through and put the rope back. "I always admired that authoritative efficiency of motion," Lewinski recalled. "The young ushers smartly dressed in their gold-trimmed maroon uniforms did not dare to stop this stern-faced father from providing his family with the best seats in the house." She had vivid memories of the view from the balcony. "The heavy luxurious gold curtains were drawn across the screen on the expansive stage," she wrote. "I remember clearly the crackle of the speakers before the movie began, the distorted images that were projected onto the folds of the curtains as they began to pull back in a ceremoniously slow dignity. We were a hushed and reverent audience poised and ready for the first pops of the speakers and chords of the Gilbert and Sullivan music that told us of refreshments in the lobby."

A majority of the time the balcony would be closed, Syfczak said. "But when we were teenagers, we'd sneak up there anyway. Ushers would chase us around." Neighborhood kids would also sneak in through the doors on Magnolia Avenue. "We'd take a coat hanger and stick it between the doors and pull the crash bar open. About ten of us neighborhood kids would scramble in and take a seat." The balcony was open for especially popular movies. "*West Side Story* was like that. *The Godfather* was like that," he said. "And when they did that, of course, they had to hire additional personnel—

ushers, candy counter girls, and all that."

Joe DuciBella worked at the Uptown when he was in high school and college, in the 1960s. Although the theater may have seemed obsolete to many observers, he saw it as bustling and vibrant. "On a Sunday, just running movies, if we didn't have ten thousand people in here, we thought business was bad," he recalled. "They tried to juggle a bunch of things, because the expense of running this building was terrific. ... Standard Oil of New Jersey, for some reason, had their stockholders' meetings here through the late 1950s."

The Uptown hosted a series of closed-circuit TV events in the 1960s, including operas and even a civil defense class conducted by officials in Washington. But boxing matches were the biggest draw. With advance ticket sales, the Uptown sold out for a broadcast of a fight on February 25, 1964, when Cassius Clay (soon to change his name to Muhammad Ali) defeated Sonny Liston in Miami Beach to become the new heavyweight champion of the world. A doorman, Harry Stahl, recalled that this was the only time he'd seen an "overflow house" at the Uptown.

In March 1964, the Uptown showed a Beatles concert filmed earlier in Washington, D.C. Terry Nelson, who was there, remembers girls screaming at the screen. This was the first chance to see the Beatles since *The Ed Sullivan Show* a month earlier. The Uptown showed the film, which included footage of separate concerts by the Beach Boys and Lesley Gore, at four matinee screenings in one weekend. Another group of British Invasion rockers, the Dave Clark Five, greeted fans at the Uptown's 1965 screening of their film *Having a Wild Weekend*—just one stop on a cinematic tour of eighteen Chicago-area theaters.

Sonny & Cher appeared at the Uptown in person in April 1967 to promote their movie *Good Times*. Maria Luisa Ugarte, who lived in the neighborhood, remembered seeing the pop duo and other rock musicians, such as Sam & Dave and Ted Nugent's band, the Amboy Dukes, who performed at the Uptown's children's matinee shows. After the Amboy Dukes played, "they ended up coming to our home on Leland, and they hung out with us," Ugarte recalled.

Outside the Uptown's doors, the neighborhood continued to change. More people of color moved into Uptown in the 1960s. By 1970, the neighborhood was 88 percent white, 5 percent Black, 4 percent Asian, and 3 percent "other," a group that included Native Americans. Overlapping those racial categories, 13 percent were "persons of Spanish language." Uptown was the city's poorest white neighborhood, with a median household income about 30 percent below the city's median.

Appalachian migrants, often blamed for Uptown's woes, decried their living conditions. "I just don't like to live in a neighborhood where your wife can't walk down the street without people's knockin' 'em in the head," said John Dawson, an Appalachian migrant quoted in the 1970 book *Uptown: Poor Whites in Chicago*. "In the spring of the year and summertime, when the weather's warm, it's just a knockout and a drag-in there. It's a gang hangout. Children usin' the language goin' up and down the streets that they use this day and time, it's pitiful. ... I think they need some recreation for the people ... places inside where it'd be warm where the children and people could go and take the kids and they could play, place of having to be in the damn streets and sidewalks in front of the cars and everything—hell, I never seen a city like this before, about that."

"There were some truly frightening aspects to Uptown," said writer and artist Emil Ferris, whose family moved to the neighborhood when she was five years old in 1967. "I saw multiple children die, and I knew of multiple children who disappeared and were found under piles of bricks. We were told not to go near the windows at night because gunshots were going off all night. There was poverty. There was alcoholism and drug addiction. There were people being let out onto the street when mental institutions were closed, who had nothing. There was cruelty of an enormous degree being done by the system." And yet, Ferris also loved Uptown: "There was this sense that people could do things. They could buck the system. There was this solidarity—a sense that we might all be falling, but we'd be holding each other's hands." Ferris drew on her childhood experiences in Uptown for her highly acclaimed graphic novel *My Favorite Thing Is Monsters* (published in two volumes in 2017 and 2024).

When Ferris saw movies at the Uptown, her father would point out architectural details and talk about the building's craftsmanship. Sitting near the front of the balcony, she felt like she might fall, overwhelmed by the sensation that she was floating in the midst of a majestic space. She witnessed kids opening exit doors to let in their friends, teens running up onto the fire escapes to get high, and drug deals inside the theater. And she attended a memorably bizarre performance at the Uptown—a brawl between Batman and Spider-Man, starring some men who looked like they'd come from the neighborhood's single-room occupancy hotels. "Appalachian white guys who were just making some money," Ferris said. "It was easier money than giving blood. They were definitely alcoholics—I could smell them. When they passed by, they were talking shit to each other. And they were performing this wrestling match.

"The outfits weren't all that great—they would sometimes pull up their pants, and their underwear was dirty. It was just insane. As kids, we absolutely loved every second of it." Ferris was fascinated by monster movies. It almost felt like she was living in one: horrors happening on Uptown's streets amid stately old buildings, most notably that massive movie palace northwest of Broadway and Lawrence. "It was Dracula's castle," she recalled. "It was the crypt. It was all of this grandeur, in a state of great decay and inhabited by monsters. It was exactly what the movies were portraying.

"And I was creeping through it with my friends, staying out as late as I could—stealing shopping carts and running them around the neighborhood, taking turns being the one in the cart and feeling the wind on my face and going past these remarkable buildings with all this romance and beauty. Feeling free and feeling wild, like a beast, like a creature. It was the most beautiful place in the world to be."

As other old movie palaces were torn down, survivors like the Uptown were looking dingy. *Tribune* reporter Edith Herman visited the Uptown in November 1968 and described its faded glory: "Dust now covers peeling gold wallpaper in the quiet balconies, and bits of cracked plaster have fallen on once colorful tapestry rugs. Many paintings, some original, still line lobby walls, but bare spots betray those stolen or sold. Gold threaded curtains hang drab beside a red velvet lobby chair with gilded arms rubbed to bare wood by thousands who sat in it waiting for films to begin. Too many handshakes from curious children have broken fingers from a white marble statue guarding the lobby fountain."

By this time, the Uptown's giant pipe organ was just a memory. Its 4,000 pipes sounded for the last time in February 1963, when Fred Arnish, who often played at roller rinks, performed one final concert on the instrument. It took four months for the Wurlitzer's new owners to haul it away. It all weighed 45,000 pounds. Traffic was blocked on several streets as the large console, with its four keyboards, was transported to west suburban Cicero. The instrument was sold to Robert Montgomery, an organist and repairman who lived in the western suburb of Cicero, and two friends from Chicago. But its pieces remained scattered for seven years, sitting in a dozen garages, basements, closets, a porch, and even a barn. In 1970, Montgomery moved it all to the Hoosier Theatre in Whiting, Indiana, where he planned to restore it and hold organ concerts. But the organ was never installed. The Wurlitzer console eventually made its way to San Jose, California, where it was installed at the California Theatre in 2004.

The Balaban & Katz chain—which owned the Uptown and 56 other theaters in Illinois and northern Indiana—was renamed ABC-Great States Inc. in 1968. "Sentimentalists are aghast at the overnight name change," *Tribune* columnist Herb Lyon wrote in 1968. "B&K is a pioneer name, maybe THE pioneer handle in the movie biz—and it does seem a shame the name of the game today is 'Drop it, switch, change it—who cares!'"

As the 1960s came to an end, many of the Uptown's artworks and furnishings went up for auction. "All the old theaters are being renovated and we no longer need these things," said company executive Raymond Fox. "We're not in the art business." The company, he explained, wanted to eliminate the cluttered feeling in its old theaters. "The ornateness has turned somewhat to being simply old-fashioned," the *Tribune* wrote.

Starting in November 1969 and stretching into 1970, the owners stripped items from the Uptown and seven other Chicago theaters (the Granada, Nortown, Chicago, United Artists, Gateway, State, and Congress). They were displayed in a series of auctions at Chicago Art Galleries, 5960 North Broadway. During the first three-day exhibition, a thousand people turned out to see what was pulled out of the theaters: paintings, rugs, torchieres, jewelry, fur coats, sterling flatware, china, light fixtures, lamps, chandeliers, and marble and bronze statues. "I'm certain that many of the people are true antique collectors looking for certain pieces," gallery owner Robert Goldstine said, "but a great many must also be looking and buying out of sheer nostalgia from those grand and ornate places that will most likely never be duplicated." He expected the gold throne chairs and bronze torchieres would be sold at a large profit for use in places such as hotel lobbies and restaurants.

The crowd at the first auction included buyers from New York and Europe. They paid up to $1,500 for marble statuettes and made five-figure bids for paintings by artists like Ralph Albert Blakelock, Cesare Agostino Detti, and Ferdinand Piloty. As the second auction approached in January 1970, the *Daily News* wrote: "Angels and cupids will descend from their starry perches in some of Chicago's most lavish old movie palaces ... landing a bit sadly on the auction block."

In 1973, Plitt Theatres bought 123 theaters from ABC-Great States, including the Uptown.

Art and furnishings were sold in 1969 and 1970.

On January 28, 1975, ads announced that the Uptown Theatre was closed for remodeling. The *Chicago Sun-Times* suggested that something else was afoot, reporting that owner Henry Plitt was "beating City Hall to the punch by closing down his Uptown movie house for renovation." Plitt Theatres actually closed the Uptown to correct alleged building code violations, according to Joe DuciBella. "A bunch of volunteers did what they could—surreptitiously, because of union reasons—to correct the violations," he said. "I can remember washing the ceiling and getting sick from the chemicals it took to wash it."

Members of the organization that DuciBella was with, the Theatre Historical Society of America, wrote letters to Plitt urging the new owners to use the theater for live entertainment in addition to movies. The Uptown reopened on March 7, 1975. And five months later, it hosted its first rock concert, initiating a new era.

CHAPTER SIX

Grateful Dead members Jerry Garcia (top), Bobby Weir, and Donna Jean Godchaux in 1978. PAUL NATKIN PHOTOS

'Both beautiful and weird.'

THE ROCK ERA

Young people flocked to Uptown in the late 1960s to experience a form of entertainment that would have shocked anyone who frequented the neighborhood back during the Roaring Twenties: rock concerts. The blaring sounds of electric guitars and drums reverberated in rooms like the Aragon Ballroom, a dramatic change from the mellow big band dance orchestras. When the Aragon's owner Andy Karzas appeared on Studs Terkel's radio show in 1963, he made clear that the curtain was closing on the ballroom era. "Young people today, the fellows don't want to learn how to dance," Karzas told Terkel. "They think it's a sissy activity. And young people go through high schools without learning. They do a lot of gyrations in record stores, but they don't learn beautiful ballroom dancing."

The Aragon shut down a year later—but reopened as the Cheetah Lounge in October 1966. White fabric covered much of the ballroom's Spanish decor. "At Cheetah, the whole place will pulse," a manager promised. After the Cheetah ran into financial trouble two years later, the place reverted back to the Aragon. And the drapes that covered the fancy decorations were removed. "Grownup people don't need all that psychedelic light-flashing to enjoy themselves," explained new owner Emerson Whitney. But they did need a new sound. This was an era of Shadows of Knight, Herman's Hermits, and Jefferson Airplane.

Over on Clark Street just north of Lawrence Avenue, the Rainbo—another venue from Uptown's 1920s heyday—also hosted rock concerts when it reopened in April 1968 as the Electric Theater. Soon renamed the Kinetic Playground, it lasted fewer than two years as a rock venue but hosted many of the era's biggest acts: Led Zeppelin, Creedence Clearwater Revival, the Byrds, Fleetwood Mac, and Van Morrison. At two shows, the Velvet Underground played on the same bill with the Grateful Dead. Another night featured the Kinks and The Who. But the Kinetic Playground closed after a fire swept through the theater on November 7, 1969, following a show by Iron Butterfly, Poco, and King Crimson.

Meanwhile, country music was the preferred genre in Uptown's many taverns, a favorite hangout for the neighborhood's migrants from Appalachia. And guitar-strumming musicians were a common sight on the streets. A few doors away from the Uptown Theatre, jazzy lounge music—often played by obscure local performers—was heard night after night in the Green Mill Cocktail Lounge, located since the 1930s in the same building that had once fronted the larger Green Mill Gardens. "I liked it when it was Uptown's most congenially seedy bar and the music was lounge-shlocky," *Sun-Times* reporter Lloyd Sachs recalled.

In 1975, an upstart company called Jam Productions began presenting concerts at the Uptown and the Riviera. Jerry Mickelson and Arny Granat founded Jam a few years earlier. "I became a promoter because I got tired of standing in line to buy tickets to shows," twenty-three-year-old Mickelson told a *Chicago Tribune* reporter in 1974. In its early years, Jam presented concerts in small venues—starting with the band War at Alice's Revisited in Lincoln Park—but the duo soon brought live music into bigger rooms, including the Aragon, where Mickelson and Granat had worked as security guards. "We were doing shows downtown at the Auditorium and the Arie Crown, and they started becoming more restrictive as to who would be allowed to play there," Mickelson recalled in a 2024 interview. Unable to book many shows at those downtown venues, Jam looked for other theaters—which led Mickelson to the Uptown and the Riviera, both just a couple of blocks from the Aragon. Jam held its first Riviera concert in April 1975, featuring Supertramp.

Mickelson, who never saw a movie at the Uptown, was stunned when he stepped inside. "You can't believe that this building is sitting here," he recalled. "It was truly spectacular—the beauty the architects designed to make you forget your cares and your troubles. It happened to be the largest capacity of any theater in the city, and everything was functioning—all the chandeliers, the heat, the air conditioning, the bathrooms." But the Uptown was not set up for concerts. "We had to make it so

PAUL NATKIN PHOTO

Bruce Springsteen on October 10, 1980, in his second Uptown concert with the E Street Band.

that the screen could move," Mickelson said. "We brought everything in—the sound, the lights, the spotlights—and staffed it with stagehands and ushers and security."

The Uptown Theatre's rock era began on October 31, 1975, when concertgoers—many of them wearing Halloween costumes—filled the theater as the Sensational Alex Harvey Band opened for the Tubes, a subversive San Francisco group who had recently released their signature tune "White Punks on Dope." The Tubes didn't just play rock songs—they also used costumes and props to perform shocking theatrical sketches. "I was tripping that night," recalled longtime Chicago concertgoer Terry Nelson. "The Tubes had this operating room scene where one of the doctors pulled out a chainsaw, jumped off the stage, and ran up the aisle—with the motor screaming and smoke pouring out of it—and all the way out of the theater. I was sitting in an aisle seat. On his way by, he whisked right over my head with it—which was quite startling to say the least." After the show, *Chicago Daily News* critic Jack Hafferkamp observed: "The Tubes seem to try hard to find something to offend everyone." But not everyone was outraged. Hafferkamp overheard one young audience member telling a friend: "The Tubes blew it, man. I heard they really used to be white punks, but now they're just like Elton John."

Sun-Times critic Al Rudis was impressed by how well the Uptown worked as a music venue when he attended a concert by Leon Russell in

PAUL NATKIN PHOTO

Bob Marley during his final Uptown concert on November 13, 1979, as part of the Survival Tour.

May 1976. "His funky music couldn't have been matched to a funkier hall than the Uptown Theatre, where you tread on years of spilled soft drinks on the way to your seat," Rudis wrote. "But at this sold-out show, it was plain to see that the Uptown is definitely superior to the Arie Crown Theater in sound and sightlines, even though it has more seats. And with a little cleaning up, it could easily approach the class of the Auditorium." Although Rudis praised the room's acoustics, he criticized the "harsh and grating" sound mixes at concerts in 1976 and 1977, blaming "sound-system gremlins" and speculating that a man running the soundboard was "probably another victim of decibel overload whose eardrums were fried long ago." Such criticisms became less frequent as time went on. "As large as it was, the sound was always great," Terry Nelson said. "It was by far the most magnificent and the largest theater I ever was in." Writing in the *Sun-Times,* Rick Kogan called the Uptown "a splendid place" for a concert by Roxy Music. "Like the group itself, it is both beautiful and weird," he wrote.

"People loved the building," Mickelson recalled. "I loved watching the fans come in and marvel at what Rapp & Rapp designed and created. When you're in a beautiful theater, it just adds a whole different element than an arena. The Uptown was the best of them all. And still is."

Some of the concertgoers Mickelson saw

lingering on the Uptown's balconies were probably experiencing the building for the first time. But one audience member at a 1977 concert by the Electric Light Orchestra was already intimately familiar with the theater and its architecture. Joe DuciBella, who had worked at the Uptown, had never seen a rock concert there. Just before ELO took the stage, the room went dark, he recalled. Lasers beamed out of the orchestra pit, pointing at architectural details all over the auditorium. "The moment was absolutely electric," DuciBella said. "Other than people being high to begin with, they just stood up and screamed. It was an absolutely fantastic moment—certainly not the original intent of the building, but it was profitable, it was fun, and everybody had a good time."

In spite of the neighborhood's scary reputation, big crowds filled Uptown to see concerts at the Uptown, Riviera, and Aragon. "Did we did we lose some people because they thought Uptown was unsafe?" Mickelson asked. "I'm sure. But I don't think the fact that it was in Uptown deterred very many people from coming. It's easy to get to with the "L." You're right off Lake Shore Drive."

Troublemakers tended to stay away from the neighborhood's concert venues, according to Dan DiSilvestro, who was one of Jam Productions' security bosses. Guards were stationed all around the theaters, along with off-duty police hired for the night. They even monitored a nearby parking garage. "We weren't being paid by anybody to make sure cars were OK in the parking lot," DiSilvestro said. "We just wanted to make sure that people felt that they could come down there. That was the difference. Can you bring daddy's car down there and it won't get heisted? They won't steal the tires off of it? People would see security there, and they would think they were pretty safe. And they were."

In the 1970s, the neighborhood's white population plummeted from about 65,000 to 30,000. Demolition, "urban renewal" projects, and widespread arson helped to spur that white exodus. Harry S Truman College opened in 1976, taking over a large chunk of the neighborhood where hundreds of run-down apartments had once stood. Almost overnight, Uptown lost its Appalachian culture.

In between the rock concerts, Plitt Theatres continued showing movies at the Uptown. In November 1976, the Chicago International Film Festival presented screenings at the Uptown, along with an appearance by Charlton Heston. Before Heston took his seat, he was warned that the chair's arms were made of flimsy foam rubber. "So what happens next? Moses comes onstage and immediately decides to sit on the arm of this seemingly solid chair," recalled Michael Kutza, the film festival's longtime artistic director. "He falls flat on his ass, stunned for only a split second before instantly pulling himself up and comfortably sitting in the chair without a word." During that same 1976 festival, the Uptown hosted the US premiere of the shocking and sexually explicit Japanese film *In the Realm of the Senses,* a month after customs officials had seized the allegedly obscene movie and prevented it from being shown in New York.

But the Uptown's days as a movie palace were drawing to a close. "Plitt wanted to unload all of their old, big old movie houses because they were basically obsolete," Mickelson said. "Plitt kept wanting me to buy it, and I was no position to buy and operate a theater at that time."

On August 18, 1978, Plitt showed its last movies—Burt Reynolds in *Hooper* and Ryan O'Neil in *The Driver*—at the Uptown. A week later, brothers Rene and Henry Rabiela took over the Uptown. The Mexican immigrants were the beneficiaries of a land trust that purchased the theater from Plitt for a price reportedly "in excess of $500,000." An anonymous Plitt spokesman told the *Tribune:* "It was all a matter of economics. Naturally, you keep theaters that are profitable and get rid of ones that are unprofitable." The Rabiela brothers had experience running other movie houses, including the Peoples Theatre in the Back of the Yards neighborhood and the Congress Theatre in Logan Square. They showed Spanish-language movies at the Uptown and held boxing matches, attracting predominantly Latino crowds

Prince opens for Rick James in February 1980. He returned as the main act in December.

while Jam Productions continued to present concerts.

Rene Rabiela Jr., who was a teenager at the time, recalled that his father was one of the first Chicagoans to receive a liquor license for a movie theater, following the Chicago City Council's 1978 decision to allow theater owners to serve alcohol. Rene remembered seeing cases of Old Style stored in the Uptown's former nursery room. "Imagine ordering fifty barrels of beer per concert, running them up maybe three, four flights—way up there—and charging about $1.50 a glass," he said. "That adds up to a lot of money. Plitt didn't have that going for them."

From 1975 through 1981, the Uptown hosted more than a hundred concerts. The headliners included well-established rock stars: Roxy Music, Lou Reed, the Kinks, Alice Cooper, Santana, and Rod Stewart. Other headliners, like Boston and Foreigner, sold out the Uptown just as they were launching their careers. Some newer stars appeared as opening acts. Billy Joel opened for Daryl Hall & John Oates in 1976. When Styx played to a rapturous crowd in 1976—greeted by rhythmic clapping and thunderous applause—the Chicago band was still a year away from its big breakthrough.

When Peter Gabriel performed at the Uptown in 1977, he'd already built a cult following as the singer for Genesis, often wearing elaborate costumes like giant flower heads. But now he was playing one of his very first concerts as a solo

Rick James and the Stone City Band on the first of two nights at the Uptown on February 28, 1980.

artist, with a simpler look. During his second encore, Gabriel shook the hands of enthusiastic fans. He returned to the Uptown the following year—shortly after Genesis had played two nights at the theater. Writing for *Rolling Stone*, Lloyd Sachs noted how Genesis relied on a "ton of special effects … to seduce their fans," including "dancing laser beams, six huge octagonal overhead mirrors and enough fake fog to stage a sequel to *Heaven Can Wait*." A week later, Gabriel "strolled down the aisle and unceremoniously hopped onto the stage." He turned a spotlight onto the crowd, looking for his band members, who joined him one by one. Later in the show, when Gabriel suddenly appeared in the audience with a cordless microphone, displaying an almost frightening intensity. "Some people were a bit wary of getting too close to him," Sachs observed.

Gabriel was friendly to teenager Rene Rabiela Jr. The teenager shared popcorn with Gabriel that night in 1978—and yet didn't recognize Gabriel in 1980, when the rock star returned with his hair shorn off. "I took a couple of my friends up to the front row to watch the sound check," Rabiela recalled. "This guy with no hair comes up to me, and he taps me on the back, and he says, 'Excuse me, don't you remember me?' I looked at him. I was like, 'No, not really.' He goes, 'I'm the guy that asked you for popcorn.' And my friends are like, 'That's Peter Gabriel!'"

Gabriel wasn't the only artist who made repeat visits. British rock band the Kinks played the Uptown five times from 1977 to 1980. "The Kinks really put on a rip-roaring show," recalled John Holden, who saw them in 1979. "It was one of the best shows I ever saw in my life." When the Kinks moved in 1981 to the bigger—and more generic—Rosemont Horizon, leader Ray Davies apologized for the change in venue, telling the audience: "I know this isn't the Uptown Theatre. But we're really trying to do our best."

Frank Zappa, another regular, appeared at the

PAUL NATKIN PHOTO

The Grateful Dead in 1979, with new keyboardist Brent Mydland during his inaugural year.

Uptown on five dates, typically playing an early concert plus a late show. The *Sun-Times* described the scene at a Zappa show in 1977: "Mom, Dad and the kids attending the concert as a family. Mom and Dad sharing a joint. Thousands cheering when Zappa ... took off his shirt. The audience throwing a 16-ounce soft drink on their hero, cup and all. ... Zappa got drenched near the beginning of the performance, just about the time he was winding up a complex guitar run. But he didn't miss a note."

No one played the Uptown more often than the Grateful Dead. The legendary psychedelic band performed seventeen concerts from 1978 through 1981, often playing three nights in a row. When Deadheads waited in line outside the theater, Jam Productions sometimes gave them rewards. Jerry Mickelson borrowed the idea from Bill Graham, the San Francisco promoter who had given roses or apples to concertgoers. "The runner that we sent out to get the roses bought the cheapest ones you could find, which meant they had thorns on them," Mickelson recalled. "And people came in with their hands cut. So, we stopped that after the first night." On another night, "we gave out apples," he said. "People started throwing them at each other, so we had to stop that."

When the Dead played at the Uptown in November 1978, Jerry Garcia met a fan named Manasha Matheson. "I was attending the concert with classmates from Shimer College," she recalled. "Our meeting at the theater was a life-changing blessing. After a long friendship, Jerry and I married in August 1990 in San Anselmo, California, where we made our home and raised our daughter Keelin."

Noah Weiner, who grew up blocks away from the Uptown, wasn't a Deadhead yet. But he later became a huge fan, listening to recordings of the Dead's Uptown concerts. "It is an agreed upon truth that 'There was never a bad show played at the Uptown,'" Weiner wrote in a blog post. "The band always went over the top." One of Weiner's favorite recordings is from the February 26, 1981, concert at the Uptown. "The 'Bird Song' on this night is spectacular," he wrote. "The solo section is propelled into a whirlwind of melting colors and throbbing suns. Music, direction, and downbeat are all consumed in an avalanche of flames, interlocked in a fractal weave. ... We have been unexpectedly thrust into a peak moment of psychedelia, where even as we shut our eyes against the madness, the visions of endlessly turning patterns glowing with lights from within consume our full attention. There is no backing away here. Jerry soars, arching over the music bed with solar flare intensity. He finds lines that arch overhead for a million miles."

Jerry Garcia spoke fondly of the Uptown Theatre in a July 1981 conversation with a journalist and some Deadheads. One of the fans told Garcia how much he loved the Uptown: "I heard about the place a lot, and then I went and saw a couple three shows there. And I was amazed at the gargoyles and the ceiling and everything. … It's beautiful." Garcia remarked: "It's a nice little theater. And it's nice that it's loose enough and relaxed enough so that people can go in there and have a good time." In that sense, it was unlike downtown Chicago's Auditorium Theatre, where the Dead also performed. The Auditorium, Garcia said, "was one of those places where you couldn't touch anything, and the audience would always get in trouble because a seat would get wrecked or something, you know? So it was, like, was really uptight, and we never sounded good in the fucking place, either." In contrast, he said, "The Uptown, like, opened up for us. It was that right combination of being basically a good theater but funky enough that nobody was worried about it. … It's a drag when the audience gets tyrannized. … It completely wrecks the whole point of it."

Mickelson knew the importance of maintaining a cool vibe. "I made sure that the security was done the way a fan would want it to be," he said. "You wouldn't want to be seeing a policeman in a uniform. You wouldn't want to see a security guard carrying a gun. You don't want to feel threatened or intimidated. You just want to go in and have a good time. But the security knew what they were doing."

That attitude extended to the way security handled the performers themselves. "Nobody hassled Jerry Garcia or the Dead or Bob Marley about smoking a joint, which is what you got at other venues," Mickelson said. "You can come in, do your show and do whatever else you do. That was OK. Just be yourself." Mickelson believed the Dead also benefited from the Uptown's policy of letting musicians control the soundboard. "At the downtown theaters, there were union regulations that were really inhibiting the band from doing their best show," he said. "The lighting director or the sound guy for the band couldn't operate the board. They had to sit next to the union guy, who they had to tell how to do it. That's never going to make a great show. At the Uptown, the deal we made with the union was: The bands will operate their boards."

During the Dead's early shows, security guards followed fire marshal orders and struggled to keep the aisles clear. "It's not possible," security boss DiSilvestro recalled. "It would be like living in a gulag. There'd be people taken out in handcuffs left and right. And I didn't see any point to that. And so, they had a long talk with the commander of the police district. After that, the security let the Grateful Dead fans do what they wanted for the most part. They wanted to be whirling dervishes. They wanted to twirl. They didn't want to rush the stage. What they wanted is to be as close to the music as they could get and dance. I was OK with that. And I finally convinced the powers that be."

The security guards were also lenient about enforcing the Uptown's rule against smoking, resulting in a cloudy atmosphere during Dead shows, DiSilvestro remembered.

Dancing fans also poured into the aisles during Bruce Springsteen's three performances at the Uptown. "His energy seems almost unbounded, and as he alternates between a wildly feral and a wholeheartedly friendly approach, he seems totally swept up in the emotion of his music," *Tribune* critic Lynn Van Matre wrote after seeing Springsteen at the Uptown in 1978. She called it "the most exciting live performance I saw in 1978." Fans still vividly remember that concert. "He had so much energy, running up and down the aisles of the theater," Brendan Towey recalled. Joe Moore, who later became a Chicago alderperson, said: "It was that Uptown concert where I transformed from a Springsteen fan to a Springsteen disciple." Another longtime Springsteen fan, Jim Bobus, said: "I'm not sure they ever matched the frenzied vibe of that show! Truly a life-changing moment for me." Rene Rabiela Jr. watched fans greet Springsteen when he emerged from a backstage door. "He signed each and every autograph before he got on his bus," Rabiela said.

Springsteen returned to the Uptown for two shows in 1980. The theater was the smallest venue on that tour for Springsteen, who remarked, "I like the intimacy of the place."

Fans lined up outside Chicago's Ticketron outlets at noon to buy tickets on the day before they went on sale. By that afternoon, a line stretched around the block outside one location in the Loop as fans wrapped in blankets and stocked with food (and, in some cases, guitars) readied themselves to endure an overnight wait. The 8,600 tickets sold out in 55 minutes.

A month later, it was showtime. "Never have I seen an audience so excited at the start of a show— standing on chairs, cheering every chord change, extending their hands toward the stage as if a single touch could save a soul," Don McLeese wrote in the *Sun-Times*. "Most of the fans had either spent a long night in line … or a lot of money with a scalper ($400 was the top asking price I heard) for a chance to see Springsteen, and they were determined that the night would be worth it. There was a lot of faith in 'The Boss' at the Uptown." Springsteen opened the show with a powerhouse version of "Born to Run," kicking off what McLeese called "more than two hours of rock 'n' roll at its most ecstatic." Of all the concerts DiSilvestro saw during his years handling security at the Uptown, Springsteen's shows were the most thrilling. "He really got into partying when he did his encore," DiSilvestro said. "It was like having him in your living room. He blended in old rock 'n' roll songs. He made you feel like your youth and his youth were the same. His personality made you feel like you were at his party."

Van Matre interviewed Springsteen in his upstairs dressing room after one of these shows. It was almost 2 a.m., and a dozen fans were waiting near the Uptown's stage door, hoping for a chance to see the Boss. Springsteen smiled, sipping tea from a Styrofoam cup, as the groupies burst into song, belting out "Born to Run" from below. "When I'm onstage, it's like, hey, it doesn't matter what happens tomorrow or what happened last night," he told Van Matre. "It's tonight that counts. I think of that kid that maybe stood in line for twelve hours to buy a ticket, and I think this is *his* night. It's me and him. This is our shot with each other."

Springsteen wasn't the only artist whose tickets were a hot commodity for scalpers. When Bob Marley played at the Uptown in 1979, tickets with a face value of $10.50 sold for as much as $25. Prices crept up during the Uptown's years as a concert venue, from a top cost of $7.50 in 1975 to $12.50 in 1981. Adjusting for inflation, both of those prices are the equivalent of roughly $40 in 2025. Some concerts cost a little more, like Rod Stewart's 1979 shows, which sold for up to $15. Like Springsteen, Stewart could have filled a bigger venue, but he opted to play at the Uptown.

Different crowds showed up for different concerts at the Uptown. After a Grateful Dead show, McLeese said he saw "more fresh flowers than anywhere this side of Amling's, and enough bandana-ed heads to give the look of an Aunt Jemima revival." When the Bay City Rollers played the Uptown in 1976, the *Sun-Times* described "females flinging themselves across the aisles." During a 1979 show by the Knack, Van Matre saw girls who "could barely contain themselves, shrieking and arguing over which member of the band was the cutest." Springsteen was, of course, also a subject of adoration: "A female fan stealthily wriggled onstage, sprinted purposefully toward her prey, and managed to quickly embrace Springsteen before jumping back into the crowd," Van Matre reported in 1980. When the Rossington Collins Band—featuring former members of Lynyrd Skynyrd—played at the Uptown in 1980, the audience supplied the vocals for a memorial "Free Bird" during the encore. "No one stood at the main microphone and only the audience sang the song," concertgoer Bob Kelly recalled. "It was a rock 'n'

Rod Stewart on May 2, 1979, on the Uptown's stage, which he demanded be painted red.

roll moment." And when Bob Marley played the Uptown in 1978, the *Sun-Times* described the crowd as "a heartening succotash of young whites, blacks, and expatriate Jamaicans" who greeted the reggae star with "unfettered admiration." But a low point was the night when barely any audience showed. Writer Rick Kogan estimated a mere fifty people, maybe a hundred, were inside the vast Uptown for the WLUP "Chicago Rocks" showcase that spotlighted ten local bands. "Where were you, you who so proudly claim that 'Chicago rocks'?" Kogan wrote in the *Sun-Times*. "Shame on you. All of you. Burn your T-shirts and turn off your radios. If Friday night's concert was any indication, you are all a bunch of phonies."

A big audience did turn out when Prince played in December 1980. "Black punk rockers, adoring female fans, hard rockers and just plain freaks of all colors and sexual preferences became the 'show' that came to watch the show," Richard Mitchell wrote in the *Chicago Defender*. Prince had made his Chicago debut ten months earlier, stealing the show when he opened for Rick James at the Uptown. Now that Prince was headlining, the multifarious crowd greeted him with rapturous appreciation.

"The sound was so deafening, it took the crease out of my pants," Mitchell wrote. "All the energy that is Prince thundered from the stage, igniting all who came to ogle, fingerpop and get off with the music. ... As Prince stood there undulating in his jet-black briefs, legwarmers and boots; he became the 'Sexy Dancer' he sang about." Years later, Prince recalled these concerts, answering journalist Jake Austen's questions with an all-caps email in 2012: "WE'RE NOT 1 2 REMINISCE

BUT WE ALWAYS GOT THE AUDIENCE WE DESERVED AND THAT TIME WAS PRETTY WILD. CHICAGO IS A MUSIC TOWN. ... THEY HAVE SEEN THE BEST AND EXPECT NOTHING LESS."

The excitement of some concerts seemed to be affecting the Uptown Theatre itself. People noticed the balcony flexing under the weight of dancing audience members. When John Holden was sitting in the balcony for the Kinks' show in 1979, "much of the crowd was jumping up and down and dancing in their seats," he recalled. "The whole balcony was shaking, and I remember wondering if there was any chance the balcony would collapse." Other people have shared similar memories online about Grateful Dead and Bruce Springsteen shows. Keith Kalafut, who worked as a security guard, recalled Frank Zappa urging the audience to jump up and down. Kalafut was standing in the balcony's front row and felt it moving. DiSilvestro saw the balcony bending at a number of concerts—especially during encores, when people were dancing in unison. Standing in the balcony, "You would feel an elevator kind of a feeling—you know, when the elevator drops," he said. DiSilvestro was also worried when he saw chunks of plaster falling from a stairwell ceiling.

According to Mickelson, the Uptown's wide balcony was designed to be flexible. "This flexibility prevents cracking or damage under stress, such as when a large crowd moves or reacts in unison," he said. He described the Uptown Theatre's structure as "pretty solid," noting that it was built with more steel than was considered necessary. "Back in the late '70s a structural engineering company was hired, and they informed us the theater is safe after studying the balcony," Mickelson said. "The swaying is well within safety limits. Engineers carefully calculate the load capacity and vibration behavior of theater balconies to ensure they remain stable under expected conditions. While it might feel a little queasy, it's a normal and safe characteristic of large, elevated structures."

Even if the Uptown's structure remained solid, other aspects of the theater needed upkeep. Don Helgeson, the longtime member of the projectionists' union, described the Uptown as "a low-budget operation," especially during the Rabiela years.

The Uptown's movie career came to an end in the first week of December 1981, when the theater showed a comedy called *Picardía Mexicana Número Dos* ("Mexican Mischief Number Two") along with the romantic drama *La Playa Vacía* ("The Empty Beach"). Those may have been the final movies at the Uptown, whose name disappeared from the Spanish-language movie listings in the *Sun-Times*. Mickelson said he received a call a few days before the J. Geils Band was scheduled to play a concert on December 19, 1981. The Rabiela brothers told him they couldn't afford to buy oil for heating the Uptown. "So we had to buy the oil to put it in the furnaces to heat the theater," Mickelson recalled. "And then when I got there on that day, the bathrooms were barely functioning." He remembered telling the Rabielas, "Either you fix this or you've got to close it."

Concert photographer Paul Natkin recalls there was no heat in the building for the J. Geils Band concert. "Everybody walked in with snow on their shoes, and the snow melted. It all rolled down the aisles and formed a lake in front of the stage. I was kneeling in it for two hours." The band members changed clothes in their bus because the dressing rooms were too cold, Natkin said. And when they played their hit song "Centerfold," they brought some Playboy Bunnies from Chicago's Playboy Club onstage. "It was 40 degrees there," Natkin said. "Let's put it this way: They were very aroused."

In spite of the challenging conditions, the group played with energy. "The crowd was on its feet from the start, dancing, clapping and carrying on as a natural reaction to the energy of the music," Don McLeese wrote in the *Sun-Times*. "If, as rumored, this was the last rock show to be held at the Uptown (at least for a while), the hall went out in a blaze of glory." That rumor turned out to be true. The Uptown Theatre went dark. At least for a while? That "while" has stretched into more than four decades.

Peter Wolf (top) of the J. Geils Band with "Centerfold" Bunnies on December 19, 1981. Bottom: Using Paul Natkin's camera, Wolf snaps a photo of happy fans from the front of the stage.

CHAPTER SEVEN
IN LIMBO

'Its beauty masked by years of neglect.'

JACK MILLER PHOTO

The Grand Lobby and its boarded-up windows from beneath the staircase.

A one-page paper message in Spanish was taped to the Uptown Theatre's box office window in March 1982: "No hay función cerrado temporalmente." *No show. Closed temporarily.*

Phil Bohmann, who had been a union projectionist at the Uptown for more than 20 years, had begun visiting the theater as a volunteer, turning the heat on and off while making sure the doors were locked. "I just want to keep it from freezing," the 80-year-old Bohmann told a *Tribune* reporter. "I do it just because I love the old theater." He declared: "The Uptown is the finest movie theater ever built. It took everything into consideration. There's not a bad seat in the house, and the acoustics are perfect. There's Rockwool insulation in the dome, so if there was a thunderstorm outside, you wouldn't hear it inside."

Bohmann hoped the Uptown would show movies again. "There's no substitute for the big screen," he said. "Television is just a little box. There's nothing like being in a big room and laughing with everyone else. If you get the product, you'll get the people back." But Plitt Theatres, which had regained ownership of the building from the Rabielas, had no interest in reopening it. "It's a nonoperating situation," Irwin Cohen, a company executive, told the *Tribune*. "We didn't wish it back. ... It's not economically sound to operate as a movie theater. ... Our concentration is on theaters in shopping centers."

Plitt sold the building in December 1983 to an anonymous land trust—which was controlled by one of Chicago's most notorious landlords, Lou Wolf and business partner Kenneth Goldberg. Nearly every time Wolf's name appeared in print, he was described as a "slumlord." He was sentenced to prison in 1974 for setting fire to an apartment building—where five families were forced to flee—so that he could collect insurance money. Now that Wolf and Goldberg owned the Uptown, "They let the building not only just stay vacant, but they allowed it to deteriorate," said City of Chicago attorney Judith Frydland.

With the heat turned off, the building's roof

JACK MILLER PHOTO

In near darkness, a detail from the lobby colonnade.

drainpipes froze and burst in the early 1980s. "They had thousands of gallons of water cascading through the building," said Uptown caretaker Dave Syfczak. Waist-high water filled the basement for more than a year. Upstairs, water wrecked ornamental plaster in several places, damage that's gone without repair for decades, and destroyed one of Louis Grell's murals in the Lawrence Avenue Lobby.

Wolf allowed restoration consultant Curt Mangel inside the building in 1984. "I walked in there and saw six inches of ice coming down the grand stairs," Mangel told the *Chicago Reader*. "The boiler was broken and the pipes had burst. There

The theater's hauntingly beautiful remains fascinate the few who now enter.

were 48,000 square feet in the basement, and it was all under four feet of water. The place was just piled high with junk—sinks, pipes, stoves—someone was using it as a storage warehouse for kitchen equipment, of all things. I keep saying that God must have a good sense of humor to give the Uptown to these guys." Mangel persuaded Wolf to give him a key to the Uptown so he could start fixing up the run-down movie palace. In spite of Wolf's bad reputation, Mangel told the *Reader:* "If he says he's going to do something, consider it done. He's very honorable in his own way." But during Wolf's time as the Uptown's owner, he pleaded guilty in 1992 to criminal racketeering for failing to pay $670,000 in taxes on twenty-one properties.

The Uptown was placed on the National Register of Historic Places in 1986. And city officials began talking about designating the theater as a Chicago landmark as Mangel made plans to team up with developer Larry Mandell to reopen the Uptown. On October 2, 1991, the Chicago City Council voted to make the Uptown Theatre a protected city landmark. The ordinance optimistically stated that the Uptown was "currently being renovated and will again provide entertainment for Chicagoans and visitors to the city."

But plans to reopen the Uptown never came together. As *Tribune* theater critic Chris Jones observed, the Uptown's location may have been one factor hindering its revival. It was far away from Chicago's Loop, sitting in "a neighborhood with significant economic challenges." As the theater sat silent, the Uptown neighborhood continued to suffer from poverty and crime—and yet, the area around Broadway and Lawrence remained a hot spot for live music. The Riviera stopped showing movies and hosting concerts in late 1983, but reopened two years later, briefly transforming into a "New York-inspired" dance club. "This neighborhood is so strange and spooky," someone in the crowd told reporter Rick Kogan. "That's certainly got to be one

A panoramic view of the Grand Lobby from the Musicians' Gallery on the mezzanine level.

of the biggest burdens this place is facing. I guess they won't make people stand out on the street. … Too dangerous." In spite of such fears, crowds turned out as the Riviera returned to its status as one of the city's major venues for rock concerts. For a time, the building's owners included Lou Wolf, the same reputed slumlord who owned the Uptown Theatre. But in 2006, a company affiliated with Jam Productions bought the Riviera.

Nearby, the Aragon Ballroom kept hosting rock and pop concerts as well as entertainment geared to Latino audiences. The venue was a mainstay for Jam Productions until it was taken over by Live Nation, which sold the Aragon's naming rights in 2019 when it officially became known as the Byline Bank Aragon Ballroom. And in the building next door to the dark Uptown Theatre, the Green Mill Cocktail Lounge—which had been serving drinks and offering live music at the same spot for half a century—transformed into a world-

JACK MILLER PHOTO

renowned jazz club (and poetry slam mecca) under the management of Dave Jemilo, who bought the business in 1986. During Jemilo's early years as the club's owner, he recalled, "I had to have off-duty coppers working the corner so people wouldn't get killed as they're going to their cars."

Metal scavenging was so rampant in the Uptown Theatre in the early 1990s that the FBI got involved, trying to prevent the looting. Many of the building's light fixtures disappeared. Some of these precious items soon showed up at salvage stores, where volunteers bought them, storing them for safekeeping. Even though the building's entrances were chained shut, some trespassers got inside, using a fire exit at the balcony level. "There was a fire in the manager's office from an untended cooking fire," said Chris Carlo, a friend of Curt Mangel. The trespassers "did no stealing," Carlo said. "They just wanted to be sheltered."

Mangel, Bob Boin, Dave Syfczak and Jimmy

Wiggins were among the people who came to be known as the Uptown Theatre's "guardian angels." "If the lights were out, the boiler wouldn't start or the water was rushing in, Jimmy was the friend you called for help," Friends of the Uptown volunteer James A. Pierce wrote in a 2020 tribute to Wiggins. "He was always just a phone call away. And he came no matter what the hour or weather. ... He went to great lengths to help find and store various historic parts and pieces that will return to the Uptown when it is restored. He would travel, barter, haul—whatever it took—to help bring something back to the Uptown that belonged there."

Boin, a retired civil engineer, was a key volunteer. "After I come home from work, I'll drive to the theater and go down to the basement," he said in the 2005 documentary *Uptown: Portrait of a Palace*. "If it's time to turn the heat on, well, then I know I'm going to be there for three hours."

Volunteers persuaded Wolf and Goldberg to donate the chandeliers and decorative pieces to their nonprofit in 1992. The items were moved to the Barrington Hills mansion of Jasper Sanfilippo and to other places for storage. "That was painful for us, because part of the beauty of the building is the magnificent light fixtures," Mangel told the *Tribune*. "But we had to do it, or they would all be gone." Mangel and Mandell formed a nonprofit called the Historic Uptown Theatre Incorporated (later to become Landmark Uptown Theatre Corporation) and bought the Uptown from Wolf and Goldberg for $1.6 million in 1995. But the property also had more than $400,000 in delinquent property taxes, which allowed David Harper and Howard Weitzman to snap it up at a Cook County scavenger sale. "I had no intention of doing anything with it," Weitzman told the *Tribune*. "It was a valuable piece of property. I maybe would have torn it down, but the community didn't want it torn down." Weitzman soon sold the Uptown for "considerably less than what the property was worth," as he put it. The new owners included developer Randall Langer and his partner Rudy Mulder.

In 1996, the National Trust for Historic Preservation placed the Uptown on its list of the country's most endangered historic places. That same year, the theater made the first of its four appearances on the Landmarks Illinois list of the state's ten most endangered historic places. Langer hired Syfczak to keep an eye on the Uptown Theatre late that year. "I was a policeman, and he brought me on for security," Syfczak said. "And then he learned I was a tradesman. So, he said, 'Why don't you just bring your tools and equipment over here and work on the theater?' And I agreed to that." Thus began Syfczak's long history as one of the Uptown's caretakers. He has continued working at the theater daily for nearly three decades, even as the property went through different owners. "When the [boiler] water is running, I gotta come check on it three times a day," he said.

Syfczak was troubled by what he found at his beloved theater. "There were horrible, humid conditions for so long," he said. "There was no ventilation. You had standing water. On the stage, we had mushrooms growing out of the wooden floor. Can you believe that?" Mildew-infested carpeting in lounges had to be pulled up. And in the basement, Syfczak removed mounds of plaster debris from the floor of the lower-level men's smoking room. "Every time somebody wanted to do an event here, I'd go, 'All right, well, you gotta order a couple dumpsters to get things cleaned up,'" he recalled.

Syfczak also encountered critters inside the Uptown, including mice and pigeons. In 2001, peregrine falcons nested on a fire escape and started dive-bombing workers who were repairing and painting fire escapes. "We built them a habitat out there," Syfczak said. "I drilled holes into the doorway, and I'd look right into the nest. People from the Field Museum would come up and observe them there." Those ornithologists put ID bands on newly hatched birds and named one after Syfczak—Dave the Falcon.

Although the Uptown's doors remained closed, the public caught occasional glimpses of the theater in movies and television shows. The ornate plaster work beneath the house-right organ screen and above the exit door looks fire-scarred—a remnant of a scene filmed for the 1991 movie *Backdraft*. "They painted that black to make it look burnt," Syfczak

Left: Plywood and posters cover the entrance of the theater in 1991.
LESLIE SCHWARTZ PHOTO

said. The Uptown's main lobby served as the toy store in 1992's *Home Alone 2: Lost in New York*. Other movies filmed inside the Uptown include *I Love Trouble, Soul Survivors,* and *Transformers: Age of Extinction*. Chicago-area rock band Enuff Z'Nuff filmed the video for its 1993 song "Right by Your Side." And Regina Spektor was filmed playing her song "Black and White" on a piano inside the Uptown in a 2018 video that also showed the Joffrey Ballet's Victoria Jaiani dancing through the building. The Uptown has been used for TV shows including *Early Edition, Chicago P.D., The Chi,* and *Station Eleven*. Apple TV's 2022 series *Shining Girls,* starring Elisabeth Moss, extensively used the Uptown's lobby spaces as a rock music club as well as a 1920s cabaret. A few bits of decoration from that project were still visible years later, including touched-up paint on the walls. "It was beautiful in here," Syfczak remarked. "It was amazing what they did with this space."

"For anyone raised on mall multiplexes, stepping into the boarded-up Uptown Theatre in Chicago is like discovering the remains of a lost civilization," journalist Todd Savage wrote after taking a tour of the building in 1999. "Even with the humiliating layers of dust, water-damaged walls, and scars where opulent light fixtures once appeared, the magnificent old movie temple manages to inspire awe." Ninety-year-old Rudy Horn, the actor who performed at the Uptown, was on the same tour, pointing his cane into dark corners. "Is the merry-go-round still there?" he asked, peeking into the nursery. Horn insisted that the building needed to be saved. "If they let that go, it's a sin," he said. "You have no idea what that theater was like. There's no theater in the world like the Uptown."

By the time Horn spoke those words, even more of Chicago's old movie theaters had been demolished, including the Granada in 1990 and the Southtown in 1991. But other movie palaces and vintages theaters were returning to life. Plans to tear down the Chicago Theatre in 1982 were thwarted, and it was revived as a venue for concerts and stage plays. After shutting down in 1981, the Oriental Theatre reopened in 1998 as a house for touring Broadway shows. (It was renamed the James M. Nederlander Theatre in 2019). Thanks to massive renovations, theaters once again became a vital part of the Loop.

The Uptown remained, but in limbo. It was saved, in part, because of its gargantuan scale. "It cost too much to tear it down!" Don Helgeson wrote. And, in part, by its location. "The theater has survived because no one has wanted the property," wrote Savage. His 1999 article in *Metropolis* magazine noted that the neighborhood "seems to have weathered the worst" but was still a tough sell for developers.

"The neighborhood's definitely on an upswing again," Uptown resident and activist Joanna Asala said in the 2005 documentary *Uptown: Portrait of a Palace*. "There's more people moving in, people who are buying property, planning on being here for the long haul. They'd like to see more entertainment. I think a restored theater would bring more restaurants, more clubs, more jobs." Ric Addy, who owned the Shake Rattle & Read store next door to the Uptown Theatre, talked about the neighborhood in the same 2005 film. "There's still a lot of panhandling and prostitution and drug sales going on," he said. "But … it's a pretty solid working-class community—you know, people that work at banks, people that are cabdrivers, just about every walk of life."

Uptown was the focus of a 2001 report by the Urban Land Institute, which argued that the neighborhood needed to preserve its "rich diversity." The Washington–based research group also stated that the neighborhood would benefit by developing an entertainment district, with a revived Uptown Theatre serving as its "crown jewel." The authors wrote: "The Uptown Theatre must be restored. It is well known that this will be an expensive and difficult process needing a tremendous program of public/private cooperation to succeed. However, the theater is truly significant historically and magnificent aesthetically. It is the kind of property of which people will say: 'Can you believe that this building was nearly torn down at the beginning of the century?' Future generations will not forgive

Left: *Preservation* **magazine used this view when it declared the Uptown "endangered" in 1996.**

The Uptown lobby fountain, pictured with a statue salvaged from the lost Granada Theatre.

those who do not attend to this obligation."

For a decade, officials and developers talked about creating a tax increment financing district to help revive the Uptown Theatre and other buildings in the neighborhood. "We can't do what we want to do without the city's help," owner Randall Langer said. In Illinois, TIF districts are widely used as a tool to spur development in blighted areas. When property values rise in these zones, the resulting increase is diverted from the local units of government that would normally receive that money into a fund that can be used for specific redevelopment projects.

In June 2001, Chicago City Council members voted to establish a TIF district covering more than seventy-three acres around the corner of Lawrence Avenue and Broadway. Plan documents stated that Uptown was suffering "from vacancies, deterioration, and obsolescence," and without a boost from TIF dollars, this area "would not reasonably be expected to be developed." The plan described how Lawrence and Broadway had been "a vibrant shopping and entertainment district" decades earlier. TIF money, city planners agreed, could help this corner with a mix of entertainment, commercial, and residential properties, restoring "vitality" to the surrounding neighborhoods.

A month after that vote, the restoration efforts received a financial boost. Arts benefactor Albert Goodman, whose family had founded the Goodman Theatre, donated $1 million from his organization, the Edith Marie Appleton Foundation. He called the Uptown a "masterpiece of construction and patron comfort." The money went to a newly formed

Below the lobby, stained glass and a chandelier remain partially lit outside the men's lounge.

neighborhood-based nonprofit called the Uptown Theatre and Center for the Arts, which began negotiating to buy the property. But the group's plans to buy the theater came to naught—along with that $1 million donation—prompting local alderman Mary Ann Smith to remark, "This theater tends to attract people with stars in their eyes."

Meanwhile, members of the Friends of the Uptown—a group formed in 1998—were calling reporters with stories of falling plaster and pooling rainwater. They worried that the building was being allowed to rot. City officials took action in 2005 after Judge Daniel J. Lynch ordered repairs. "That's when the engineers came," Syfczak said. Workers removed loose sections of the theater's glazed terra cotta façade, cataloging and numbering the pieces as they were stored inside the building, so that they could someday be placed on the exterior again. Workers also replaced some of the building's massive roof drainpipes and enclosed a chimney covering a space in the attic where precious warm air had been venting. "That was the work we did to stabilize the building," Syfczak said. "The city paid the tab on all that—to remove the loose and hazardous masonry, hire an engineering firm, hire a masonry contractor."

Jerry Mickelson and Arny Granat—the Jam Productions owners who put on so many concerts at the Uptown between 1975 and 1981—made an effort to buy the theater. They formed a new limited liability company called UTA II and bought out various owners. "There were a number of entities and interests we had to purchase," said Mickelson. "It wasn't just one person." There were two mortgages with different mortgage holders, and the property

LOREN ROBARE PHOTO

A faded remnant of the old nursery.

was in foreclosure. A separate land trust possessed the property title. And the city had a lien on the property, seeking money for the repairs it had performed. As UTA II attempted to take over the Uptown, real estate investor David Husman still held one of the mortgages. "I asked him what he was going to do with the theater, and his response was he was going to turn it into an indoor go-kart track," Mickelson said. "He kept forestalling the sale."

On Mickelson's side in the litigation, attorneys Eric S. Rein and Bethany N. Schols urged a judge to take action. "A once bustling theater, among the largest movie palaces ever created, is silent; its beauty masked by years of neglect," they wrote. "But the Uptown Theatre's future could be grand; it could, once again, be a movie palace; it could once again be the heart of the neighborhood. And the path to reclaiming that former majesty is simple—take the property out of this judicial deadlock and allow a new owner to renovate the Uptown Theatre."

Judge Darryl B. Simko ordered the building to be sold. UTA II won the Uptown Theatre in a 2008 public auction, paying $3,234,880.40. Two of Jam's competitors, Live Nation Inc. and Madison Square Garden Entertainment, had looked into buying the theater, but neither company took part in the auction. "I was the only one who showed up," Mickelson said. With the purchase, Mickelson and his various businesses now owned the Uptown Theatre as well as the Riviera, Vic Theatre, and Park West.

Mickelson said he has spent $400,000 to $500,000 a year to maintain the Uptown Theatre since then, plus paying about $200,000 a year in property taxes. "I do this for the sake of saving it," he said.

Shortly after Rahm Emanuel won election as Chicago's mayor in 2011, he talked about creating an Uptown entertainment district with a revived Uptown Theatre as its cornerstone. Doing this "could drive the economy of that area with more restaurants and more other types of retail and commercial life that would really take off," he said. In October 2011, the new mayor described his reaction to stepping inside the shuttered movie palace, telling the *Tribune,* "Your jaw drops. It's stunning." But there were moments of friction between city officials and the Uptown's owners. In January 2014, city inspectors reported seeing a huge icicle in the Uptown's basement. A lawyer for ownership firm UTA II said the building's heat was off because the owners were switching from oil heating to natural gas, as the city had requested.

Emanuel's Chicago Infrastructure Trust nearly struck a deal in 2015 to buy the Uptown and turn it into a nonprofit venue for movies, concerts, and other events. The group proposed adding a large, rectangular "fly loft" structure on top of the Uptown Theatre roof, which would allow for an IMAX screen to move up and down. "One of their ideas was to divide the balcony into smaller theaters, which made me sick," Mickelson said. "I hated that idea. They would have chopped it up, and it wouldn't be the same Uptown Theatre." In the end, it didn't matter what the Chicago Infrastructure

Right: The Grand Foyer waits to be restored.
SUZY POLING PHOTO

CHRISTOPHER JACKSON PHOTO

Despite water damage and disuse, details in the Uptown auditorium provoke wonder and mystery.

Trust wanted to do. The $120 million restoration plan collapsed when Emanuel asked the group's CEO Stephen Beitler to resign, along with the staff members who had been working on the project.

Meanwhile, the city added a landmark designation to the area around the Uptown Theatre in 2016. The building itself had already been named a Chicago landmark in 1991, but now the whole Uptown Square District—including the theater as well as other historic buildings clustered around Lawrence and Broadway—achieved landmark status.

After years of talk and rumors about something happening with the Uptown Theatre, an announcement finally came on June 29, 2018, when Emanuel declared that the it would be restored and reopened. With the mayor himself vowing that the project would happen, it seemed more likely than ever before. "The restored theater will be the centerpiece of the new, revitalized Uptown entertainment district, giving residents and visitors another way to experience world-class culture and entertainment in one of the city's most storied neighborhoods," Emanuel said in a press release.

The revived Uptown would have a capacity of 5,800 during events with the main-floor seats were removed. The *Tribune* quoted Mickelson's business partner Arny Granat describing the variety of events the Uptown would host: "Concerts. Comedy. Dance. Special events. A whole multitude of things. This is a game changer for the city. It's not just about concerts—it's about the economic development that now will occur in the Uptown neighborhood."

The $75 million plan was a joint venture between UTA II and Farpoint Development, a Chicago-based company led by Scott Goodman, who previously cofounded Sterling Bay, one of Chicago's biggest real estate developers. Mickelson and Farpoint needed to come up with $26 million

CHRISTOPHER JACKSON PHOTO

Bacchus laughs in the dark atop a water fountain. Following pages: The darkened auditorium.

to $30 million to make the project happen. As the *Tribune* explained, this would be "a yet-to-be-determined mix of debt and equity." The rest of the money would come from government sources: $13 million from the TIF district, $8.7 million in federal tax credits, $3 million in Adopt-A-Landmark funds, $10 million in Build Illinois bonds, and $14 million in state government money from the Property Assessed Clean Energy Act, which uses special property assessments to pay for energy-related building improvements.

Restoration would begin in 2018 and be completed in 2020, according to the city's announcement. But the project's architects, the Lamar Johnson Collaborative firm, weren't announced until November 2018. "We're working with the parameters of the existing building," said George Halik, then a principal at Lamar Johnson. "And we're putting the money where it will be of most use, both structurally and visually." That November was also when the Chicago City Council officially authorized negotiations for a redevelopment agreement. At the time, Emanuel remarked, "Uptown was an eyesore. Now, it's going be a place for entertainment and jobs." City officials recommended a tax break for the Uptown Theatre—reducing property taxes by $2.2 million over twelve years as an incentive to restore the landmark.

Tribune theater critic Chris Jones wrote enthusiastically about the Uptown's potential: "Once it reopens ... the Uptown will be one of Chicago's biggest visitor attractions, if they get the tours right. Not only is it that cool, it has been years since anyone has seen it with their own eyes." He predicted that the revived theater would have a ripple effect in the Uptown neighborhood, attracting new music venues, galleries, and restaurants, while drawing in people from other parts of the city. But by November

2019, Jones reported that the project had stalled: Mickelson was still trying to pull together the $26 million in private financing. "The investors are kicking the tires and doing their due diligence," he told Jones, predicting that work would begin in the spring of 2020. By this time, Arny Granat had ended his partnership with Mickelson at Jam Productions, but he remained part of UTA II, the LLC that owns the Uptown.

And then the COVID-19 pandemic hit in early 2020. "Everything fell apart," Mickelson said in December 2024. "We couldn't close the deal. Everybody we were talking to pulled back—and rightfully so. That's just the way it was. Entertainment venues were the first to close." But when the pandemic subsided, business boomed for Jam Productions and other concert promoters. "It came out like gangbusters," he said. "There was pent-up demand from the fans and pent-up touring plans from the bands."

As the Uptown Theatre's 2025 centennial approached, Mickelson was trying to get its revival back on track. Speaking in December 2024, Mickelson said the project would involve "pretty much the same team" that worked on it in 2018. Mickelson updated the project's cost estimates, while Syfczak gave building tours to architects and engineers.

"The Uptown is in actually really good shape for being closed since '81," Mickelson said. "The cost of what we will incur is new electrical, new plumbing, new HVAC, new mechanicals, a new elevator. Fix the façade. All of those things are what adds up. It's not an impossible job. It's just such a large theater; it costs a lot of money. It's just a big task." Asked about the concerns some people raised about the way the balcony flexed under the weight of dancing concertgoers, Mickelson said: "Before restoration begins, another structural engineer will weigh in on the balcony."

Mickelson envisioned the Uptown as primarily a concert venue. "That's how it's going to make its mark," he said. "The Uptown is the largest of all the theaters in the city. We'll take the seats off the main floor and tier the floor so that we can do general admission shows." At other shows, folding chairs will be placed on the main floor for reserved seating. The Uptown's spacious lobbies could also be used for other events. "It's perfect for weddings," Mickelson said—and he should know. He got married in the theater's lobby after buying the

ABOVE AND PREVIOUS PAGES: CAREY PRIMEAU PHOTOS

Above the Grand Foyer, where crowds used to gather on their way to balcony seats.

building.

Mickelson said he doesn't want to make any radical changes in the Uptown Theatre. As he sees it, Rapp & Rapp achieved perfection. "They designed their auditoriums so they were wide, and that allowed for the last row to never be too far from the stage," he said. "Their balconies are so close to the stage. They figured that out. They figured out the acoustics. They figured out the curves of the ceiling. They knew about flow and traffic and getting people in and out. They were masters at that."

Mickelson pointed to the work Jam

Almost to the top of the balcony, fallen plaster litters the steps near the seventh level.

Productions has done in recent years to restore original design elements of the Riviera. "I like to restore the theaters to the way they were," he said. "At the Riv, I found the original floor tile in the bathrooms," he said. "I found the wall tile. I matched it. I uncovered original windows that were covered with plywood. I took steel plates off [the stair treads] and found these beautiful marble stairs." Syfczak said he hopes similar restoration work could continue inside the Uptown even after it reopens. Every single thing doesn't need to be fixed up before the place reopens. "You watch your budget," he said. "What can we include?"

Critics have wondered how a revived Uptown

CAREY PRIMEAU PHOTO

Theatre would fit into Chicago's current landscape of entertainment venues. The skeptics include concert photographer Paul Natkin, who questions how many musical acts would actually play at the Uptown. Artists who are popular enough to fill the Uptown may choose instead to play at even bigger venues, such as Soldier Field or Tinley Park's Credit Union 1 Amphitheatre, he said. "You've got to have a certain amount of shows there to keep the place open," Natkin said. "I hope they fix it up. It was a great place to go to hear a concert. But I can't see the economics of it working."

However, Mickelson said the Uptown could host concerts by artists who would sell out somewhat smaller spaces, like the Chicago Theatre, the Auditorium Theatre, the Salt Shed, the Rosemont Theatre, the Arie Crown Theater, and the Aragon Ballroom. (With reserved seating, the Uptown's capacity is smaller than the Aragon's, but it would hold more people when main-floor seats are removed.) A band that sells out two nights at the 2,500-capacity Riviera Theatre could perform for the same number of people in a single night at the Uptown. "There are a lot of venues in Chicago that will all be competing for the same talent," Mickelson said. He doesn't see that as a problem. But in early 2025, as plans moved ahead for a 6,000-seat concert hall near the West Side's United Center, Mickelson echoed the sentiments of a *Tribune* editorial headlined: "West Loop Entertainment District Should Not Come at the Cost of Historic Venues Such as Uptown Theatre." Said Mickelson: "The city should have a plan in place to protect and preserve their historic old theaters ... so new sterile theaters cannot be built. Why should the city allow a zoning variance for any proposed new theater if it will affect our city's architectural gems?"

Even as the Uptown Theatre sits dark, the area around Lawrence and Broadway often buzzes with concert activity at the Riv, Aragon, and Green Mill. It's common to see concertgoers forming long lines on the sidewalks. Not far away, the Double Door—a rock venue that closed in Wicker Park in 2017—announced plans to reopen inside the old Wilson Avenue Theatre, which spent most of its life as a bank. Mickelson said he expects there will be nights in the future when the Uptown, the Riv, and the Aragon all have concerts at the same time. Some people say that will create a parking nightmare in the neighborhood, but Mickelson isn't worried. "It's never been a problem," he said, suggesting that people could park at existing lots and garages in the neighborhood or take public transportation or use ridesharing services.

At the start of 2025, Mickelson was seeking assurance from city officials that the Uptown would get TIF money. Uptown's TIF district was originally scheduled to expire at the end of 2025, but the City Council voted to extend it until 2037. "The big ask here is the TIF money," Mickelson said. "Once I know what that is or isn't, then I can go out and try and raise the money." He insisted the project wouldn't be feasible without a public-private partnership. "If the private sector has to put up too much money, it can't work. The return just doesn't make any sense," he said. "There's always going to be years when you have a downturn, so you can't be too leveraged. If I had been too leveraged at the Riv, Vic, and Park West, I'd be out of business. Bad times can happen anytime. You've just got to be careful."

Mickelson suggested that the Uptown project would benefit from philanthropy.

"It might require the benevolence of Chicagoans who want to save this theater, that have the wherewithal to make a donation just to save this historic building. … I've been doing it all myself, with my partner, and it's a daunting task. We're not the wealthiest people in the world. We'll put our money up, but we can't do it ourselves."

Like any project involving government financing and incentives, the Uptown has sparked questions about whether it deserves such support. The project's advocates argue that it would boost the neighborhood's economy. While the Uptown Theatre sat unused for more than four decades, the neighborhood around it evolved. It has not yet enitrely shaken off its reputation as a place that is a bit scarier, weirder, and grungier than other areas of Chicago's North Side, but it is not as poor or as violent as it used to be. Now, Uptown has fewer people living in poverty. Uptown's progressive voices worried that gentrification was pushing out longtime residents who couldn't afford rising rents.

The Lawrence-Broadway TIF district helped to pay for some of the changes in Uptown, including the renovations of the Uptown Broadway Building and the former Goldblatt's Department Store

block, both about a block south of the theater. That complex encompasses the original Sheridan Trust and Savings Bank and the five-story Loren Miller & Company department store, which gave the Uptown neighborhood its name. The neighborhood has experienced a construction boom, with new

CAREY PRIMEAU PHOTO

Though its last performance was decades ago, the theater still inspires awe.

residential buildings going up while renovations revive older structures.

Meanwhile, Uptown's transit infrastructure received an upgrade. The Chicago Transit Authority spent $203 million building a much larger and more modern station for the Red and Purple Lines at Wilson Avenue before embarking on a similar project to demolish and rebuild the Lawrence Avenue station.

So, Uptown is not exactly the same as it was back when city officials created the TIF district in 2001. Does the neighborhood still need tax increment financing to encourage development? Mickelson argued that it's essential for reopening the Uptown Theatre, which was one of the original goals for the TIF district in 2001. The Lawrence-Broadway TIF district had a fund balance of $39.6 million at the start of 2024—money that could potentially be spent on the Uptown Theatre and other neighborhood projects.

Mickelson described how a reopened Uptown Theatre would benefit the public. The theater could provide jobs and opportunities for young people. He said he would provide it as a free space for community events and education, working with groups like the People's Music School, the Merit School of Music, and Chicago Public Schools. "I'm going to make a deal with CPS to have their kids come in and learn about front-of-house and back-of-house activities," Mickelson said. "I want to open up their eyes to what they can do."

Behind the locked doors of the Uptown Theatre, Dave Syfczak is still patrolling the lobbies and corridors in 2025, almost three decades after he first took on his role as the building's caretaker. By his count, the theater has gone through five owners, although Mickelson's partnership has owned it for most of those years. "I just kind of hung in there," Syfczak says. "I'm still here."

A century after it opened, the Uptown Theatre sits dark and silent. It hasn't had any light bulbs shining on its façade and marquee since December 1981. Plywood and padlocks block the entrances where throngs of thrill-seekers once passed. Only a small number of Chicagoans can say they've been in the building over the past forty-four years. Inside, the Uptown has lost its original furnishings and artworks. Some were removed by the theater's owners and auctioned off. Others disappeared under mysterious circumstances. Some chandeliers and fixtures are stored elsewhere for safekeeping, waiting for the day when the Uptown Theatre opens and welcomes crowds back.

As time passes, the price for reopening the Uptown continues climbing higher, with cost estimates now exceeding $100 million.

In spite of everything, the Uptown Theatre retains its grandeur and magnificence. The architectural genius of Rapp & Rapp is intact. The theater's dimly lit interior is scuffed up, but the size and shape of its spaces are still awe-inspiring. In parts of the building, gaping holes in the walls are visible, scars from the early 1980s when roof storm drains froze and burst, destroying sections of decorative plaster. Those pipes have long since been replaced, but the damage remains. The vast majority of the Uptown's decorative plaster is still in place. Countless grotesque faces peer out from the walls and corners.

Owner Mickelson calls it "the eighth wonder of the world." As this book was being written in 2025, he sounded hopeful that something might happen.

"When they opened the theater in 1925, they designed these palaces to have the person going to the movie forget their troubles and cares," Mickelson says. "They were designed to take you to a different place. And that still happens today when you walk in there. ... The Uptown is the nicest. It needs to be saved, because it will never be built again. You need to save this for future generations to see. The point is: Save it. Get it open. And let it do its magic."

A hundred years ago, a Balaban & Katz advertisement called the Uptown Theatre "architecture like 'frozen music,' sculpture of heroic size, elegance beyond all your dreams." The ad was quoting German author Johann Wolfgang von Goethe, who famously remarked, "I call architecture a frozen music." As Goethe said, "The mood that emanates from architecture comes close to the effect of music." His turn of phrase, translated into ad copy, feels like an even more fitting description of the Uptown Theatre in 2025. The theater may not be literally frozen (as it was for a while in the early 1980s, when it survived without heat), but as an entertainment venue and public building, it has been frozen in time for nearly half of its existence.

And yet, its architecture is as musical as ever. Balaban & Katz's copywriters declared the Uptown "a thing that comes miraculously seldom." And now, it sits—waiting for another miracle.

Right: "Beyond Human Dreams of Loveliness." Following pages: The shuttered bronze entrance doors.

Notes on Sources

I constructed this history from a variety of building materials, including numerous old documents as well as the memories of people, both living and dead, who played a part in the Uptown Theatre's story. More than 500 articles and advertisements from Chicago newspapers and *Variety* magazine revealed essential details about key moments at the Uptown over the past century.

Descriptions of the Uptown include details from the 1986 form nominating the theater for the National Register of Historic Places that was prepared by Donald K. Lampert and Leonard D. Williams. Other descriptions come from *Balaban & Katz Magazine*'s August 17, 1925, issue; *Marquee* magazine's special Uptown Theatre issue, published in 1977; an essay by Arthur Frederick Adams, courtesy of his family's archives; and blueprints in the Chicago History Museum's collection of Architectural Records for Buildings by Rapp & Rapp.

Sources for the early history of the Uptown neighborhood include Harold Charles Hoffsommer's 1923 Northwestern University master's thesis "The Development of Secondary Centers Within Metropolitan Cities: 'The Wilson Avenue District,' Chicago"; the Commission on Chicago Landmarks' 2016 designation report for the Uptown Square District; Michael Glover Smith and Adam Selzer's 2015 book *Flickering Empire: How Chicago Invented the US Film Industry*; Loren Miller's May 1921 article in *System: The Magazine of Business* "You Can't Sell Against That Competition"; Ernest R. Mowrer's 1927 book *Family Disorganization: An Introduction to Sociological Analysis*; Edwin Balmer's 1925 novel *That Royle Girl*; Ben Hecht's story "Nirvana," published August 23, 1921, in the *Chicago Daily News*; and census documents from the U.S. Census Bureau website and Ancestry.com.

Information on property transactions involving Green Mill Gardens, the Riviera Theatre, and the Uptown Theatre comes from records at the Cook County Clerk's Office Recordings Division. Details about the construction of these buildings are from city building permits digitized by the University of Illinois Chicago Library. Other facts about Green Mill Gardens were found in Clerk of Cook County Circuit Court Archive's documents for the probate case for Charles E. Morse's estate (4-8818, 1908) and the lawsuit *Tom Chamales v. Catherine Hoffman et al* (B180140C, 1929). For more documentation—and more stories—see my online history project "The Coolest Spot in Chicago: A History of Green Mill Gardens and the Beginnings of Uptown" at robertloerzel.com.

The history of Balaban & Katz is based on Carrie Balaban's 1942 book *Continuous Performance: The Story of A.J. Balaban*; "As to A.J. Balaban" by Sime Silverman in *Variety*, February 27, 1929; *American Hebrew*'s April 6, 1928, story about Sam Katz, "Like a Movie Story"; David Balaban's 2006 book *The Chicago Movie Palaces of Balaban and Katz*; William R. Weaver's January 1932 *Chicagoan* article "Movie of a Movie"; and Douglas Gomery's 1992 book *Shared Pleasures: A History of Movie Presentation in the United States*. W.A.S. Douglas's comments are from his October 1927 *American Mercury* essay "The Passing of Vaudeville." Adolph Zukor's quotation is from the 1953 memoir he wrote with Dale Kramer, *The Public Is Never Wrong: The Autobiography of Adolph Zukor*. The quotations by Barney Balaban, structural engineer Ernest Lieberman, and architect A.J. Mayger are from their testimony in the 1928 lawsuit *Balaban & Katz Corporation v. Commissioner of Internal Revenue*.

Details about Rapp & Rapp were drawn from Charles Ward Rapp's 2014 book *Rapp & Rapp: Architects*. Sources for the history and architecture of movie palaces include Ben Hall's 1961 book *The Best Remaining Seats* and Maggie Valentine's 1994 book *The Show Starts on the Sidewalk: An Architectural History of the Movie Theatre, Starring S. Charles Lee*. Information about various theaters came from the Cinema Treasures website and *Marquee*'s 1991 list of "Motion Picture and Vaudeville Theatres of the United States Over 2,800 Seating Capacity." Comments on the Garrick Theatre were pulled from editor John Vinci's 2021 book *Reconstructing the Garrick, Adler & Sullivan's Lost Masterpiece*.

Balaban & Katz's policies and employee instructions are from two books that the company published in 1926: *The Fundamental Principles of Balaban & Katz Theatre Management* and *Training of Theatre Employees for Balaban & Katz Service*. Chapter 4's schedule for a day at the theater is based on a 1926 document reproduced in *Marquee*'s 1977 special Uptown issue. Information on Frank Cambria is from the March 26, 1927, article he wrote for *Moving Picture World*, "Evolution of Presentation in Motion

Pictures," and Thomas C. Kennedy's June 3, 1927, *Motion Picture News* article "Frank Cambria Discusses Theatre Design and Decoration."

Reminiscences about the Uptown were drawn from articles including Robert Marsh, "Critic At-Large: Console Comeback," *Chicago Sun-Times*, February 14, 1963; Edith Herman, "Staff of Aging Gilt Movie Palace Recalls Glories of the Old Days," *Chicago Tribune*, November 14, 1968; Cara Jepson, "Memories of a Trouper," *Chicago Reader*, June 12, 1997; and Jo Lewinski, "Memories of the Uptown Theater," *Nostalgia Digest*, Spring 2003.

The mob's involvement in the projectionists' union was documented in Gus Russo's 2001 book *The Outfit: The Role of Chicago's Underworld in the Shaping of Modern America* and David Robb's September 1, 2015, *Deadline* article "Mob Relatives Drawing Pensions from Chicago IATSE Projectionists' 'Endangered' Plan."

The removal of the Uptown's organ was told in "Aging Theater Pipe Organ to Entertain Once Again," *Berwyn Life*, July 24, 1963; Sherry Fyte's article "Pipe Organ Gets a Home," (Hammond, Indiana) *Times*, March 20, 1970; and Bob Shomler's 2017 blog post "California Theatre Organ Console," shomler.com/calsj/console.htm.

The later history of the Uptown neighborhood is based on sources including Todd Gitlin and Nanci Hollander's 1970 book *Uptown: Poor Whites in Chicago*; Mark Guarino's 2023 book *Country and Midwestern: Chicago in the History of Country Music*; the Urban Land Institute's 2000 report *Uptown Chicago, Illinois*; and Chicago Community Area Data on Rob Paral & Associates' website, robparal.com. Michael Kutza's story is from his 2002 memoir *Starstruck: How I Magically Transformed Chicago Into Hollywood for More Than Fifty Years*. Jerry Garcia's comments are from the audio of his July 10, 1981, interview with Greg Harrington posted at archive.org/details/jg1981-07-10-Interview.shnf. Noah Weiner's writing is from the Dead Listening website, deadlistening.com.

The history of the Uptown since it closed in 1981 is indebted to reporting by Mark Caro, Chris Jones, Blair Kamin, Stevenson O. Swanson, Jon Anderson, and Ryan Ori of the *Chicago Tribune*; Jim DeRogatis, William Smith, and Fran Spielman of the *Chicago Sun-Times*; Mark Guarino, Greg Hinz, and Eddie Baeb of *Crain's Chicago Business*; Ben Joravsky and J.R. Jones of the *Chicago Reader*; and Todd Savage, whose article "Moving on Uptown?" ran in *Metropolis* magazine in December 1999. Other sources include Cook County property documents and the Cook County Circuit Court cases *People v. Michael J. Morrison* (2002-CH-08223) and *Associated Bank Chicago et al v. Standard Bank Trust Company et al* (2003-CH-07967.)

Jerry Mickelson and Dave Syfczak's comments are from my interviews and email exchanges in late 2024 and early 2025. I also interviewed Dan DiSilvestro, Emil Ferris, Don Helgeson, Dave Jemilo, Keith Kalafut, Paul Natkin, and Maria Luise Ugarte and exchanged messages with John Holden, Terry Nelson, and Jay Sutphin.

Manasha Garcia and Chris Carlo's comments are from emails with James A. Pierce. This book also includes comments Joe DuciBella and Rene Rabiela Jr. made during a circa 2000 tour of the Uptown Theatre documented on video as well as comments that Bob Boin, Joanna Asala, and Ric Addy made in the 2006 documentary film *Uptown: Portrait of a Palace* by John Pappas and Michael Bisberg. The book quotes letters that Charlene Adamski, Constance A. Coultry, Tony DiMartino, Don Helgeson, Bob Kelly, Eileen Levine, and Rose Wandel wrote to the Uptown Theatre History Project and Friends of the Uptown between 1998 and 2002 (collected by Pierce), as well as Facebook messages posted by Jim Bobus, Al Katz, Sean McDermott, Joe Moore, and Brendan Towey.

— Robert Loerzel

Photo Notes

This book would not have been possible without historical photographs provided by the Theatre Historical Society of America. These include the images on pages 2-3, 23, 25, 26, 27, 28, 29, 31, 34, 37, 38, 39, 40, 41, 42, 43, 46, 47, 49, 50-51, 52, 53, 54-57, 58, 59, 79, 80-81, 82, 84, 85, 89, 93, 96-97, 104 and 105.

Additionally, seven photographs were provided by the Chicago History Museum. They are:

Page 30: ICHI-189043	Page 36: ICHI-189045
Page 32: ICHI-189047	Page 44: ICHI-189042
Page 33: ICHI-189048	Page 48: ICHI-189046
Page 35: ICHI-189044	

Acknowledgments

We are grateful for support from the Richard H. Driehaus Foundation, Classic Cinemas, the Jerry Garcia Foundation, Preservation Chicago, the Sanfilippo Foundation, Alderperson Angela Clay (46th Ward), and Landmark Uptown Theatre Corporation.

Thank you to the Chicago History Museum, Chicago Transit Authority, Chicago Tribune, Theatre Historical Society of America, Snapshot Nation, Vicki Granacki, Perry Casalino and Phil Robare for the use of historic photographs as well as photographers Richard Cahan, Christopher Jackson, Barbara Karant, Paul Merideth, Jack Miller, Mark Montgomery, Paul Natkin, Eric J. Nordstrom, Suzy Poling, Carey Primeau, Loren Robare, Leslie Schwartz, and Bob Shomler.

And thanks to Art Adams and Devin Baker, for access to the collection of Arthur Frederick Adams, chief of design for Rapp & Rapp; Joanne Asala and Ted Calhoun, for the use of historical artifacts; Beth Eckerty, for unwavering encouragement; David Gans, for sharing the mythology of the Grateful Dead; Manasha and Keelin Garcia, for their spirit and interest in saving the Uptown; Matt Galo and Matthew Kulju, for legal advice; Albert Goodman, for decades of support; Leigh Hanlon, for editing; Curt Mangel, for work and wisdom; Jerry Mickelson, for stewardship and enthusiasm; Charles Ward Rapp, for sharing his family's collection; Patrick Seymour, for expert assistance with the Theatre Historical Society of America archives; Dave Syfczak, for tireless dedication and faith; Brian Wolf, for research and editing, and Bradford White.

This book is in memory of Phil Bohmann, Bob Boin, Joe DuciBella, Joyce Dugan, Peter Miller, Loren Robare, Richard Sklenar, Jasper and Marian Sanfilippo, Mary Ann Smith, Jimmy Wiggins, and Dennis Wolkowicz.

What remains of the Uptown vertical sign.

RICHARD CAHAN PHOTO